CC

TANGO DOWN THE CORRIDOR

by
Joan Gordon

Everyone has a story to tell. We find ways of helping them tell it

Yorkshire Art Circus
1991

Published by Yorkshire Art Circus
School Lane, Glasshoughton, Castleford
West Yorkshire WF10 4QH
Telephone (0977) 550401

© Joan Gordon
Edited by Brian Lewis and Joan Thornton
© Cover design by Tadpole Graphics

ISBN 0 947780 68 8 $942 \cdot 8 \cdot 9$
Classification: Autobiography

Typesetting by Print Assist, Castleford

Printed by FM Repro Ltd., Repro House, Lumb Lane, Roberttown,
Liversedge, West Yorkshire WF15 7NB   Tel (0924) 411011

Yorkshire Art Circus is a unique book publisher. We link our books
with performances and exhibitions and offer workshops for the
first time writer. Yorkshire Art Circus projects have successfully
toured community centres, colleges, galleries, galas, clubs and art
centres. In all our work we bring new artists to new audiences.

For details of our projects send for our brochure and book list to
the address above.

Yorkshire Art Circus is a non-profit making limited company,
currently seeking charitable status.

Acknowledgements

Rachel Adam	Olive Fowler	Joan Thornton
Pam Davenport	Brian Lewis	Rachel Van Riel
Margaret Edwards	Reini Schühle	

**We would like to thank the following organisations for support
towards this book:**

Tango
Down The
Corridor

Chapter One

When Nurse Lilley had departed, Auntie Ida came round to cheer Mother up and brought Jeffrey and Rex, her two younger sons, with her. They were both happy children, always beaming. Once I copied them and tried to pee standing up. They rolled about laughing. Mother was not amused.

Jeffrey was to stay the night now Mother was well enough to cope. Mother stood over me while I ate a boiled egg and drank up a beaker of milk for tea and as I hated both I was fuming. Then we were both put to sleep in her double bed with a bolster down the middle, which made me crosser still. In order to see Jeffrey, I had to sit up. I wanted to do the most awful thing I could think of but I didn't dare.

'I'll give you a toffee and a look at my bottom, if you'll wet the bed,' I said. Jeffrey haggled for two toffees then the deal was struck. I fell asleep pleased with my revenge. Until next morning when Auntie Ida heard about it and raised her normally quiet voice to Jeffrey, 'How could a big four-year-old like you do such a thing!' My conscience stung then as I thought he was in for a smack. He didn't give me away but I was sure Mother would find out. Grown-ups usually did. For days I was subdued, expecting retribution.

Nothing happened until the following week. I was collected by Auntie Ida to play with the boys but when I was taken home I found Mother had gone. Mrs Wiles was there to put me to bed but only gave me a hurried wash. I was too devastated to cry. Would Dad come home or had he gone as well? To my relief he came before Mrs Wiles had left, gave me a quick goodnight kiss but told me nothing of Mother's whereabouts. I was too scared to ask in case she had died. I felt somehow responsible and laden with guilt. The next day Dad shaved in silence. He did not invite me in to watch.

I was left with Mrs Wiles, who gave me a helping of Force flakes, which I detested, even though they were in my favourite dish. I loved that dish, because as I ate up the mush, the Queen was gradually revealed with red and blue robes and her crown askew. But that day even the first mouthful tasted of ashes.

While Mrs Wiles cleaned the house I had to amuse myself. It was August, but chilly, so I sat all day long crouched in front of the fireguard looking into the flames. On Sunday, Dad took me for a walk in the park but there was little conversation. We were both locked in our own misery.

A week later, a card came through the letterbox and it was handed to me. I had only had cards before on my birthday. This one had a Mabel Lucie Atwell picture on the front, of a child paddling. 'It's from Mummy,' Dad said and my heart leapt. So she was alive!

'She's at Brighton,' Dad added. 'She says *Feeling much better, see you soon. Lots of love, Mother.*'

Brighton meant paddling, collecting pebbles and playing on the beach. I'd been taken there the previous year so I knew what I was missing. How could Mother have gone without me? I now felt murderous as well as miserable. From then on each day dragged like a year.

On Saturday two weeks later Dad dressed me in my best coat, patent leather ankle-strap shoes and last pair of clean socks. Then we went on the tram to the station to meet Mother. As the train thundered in I was scared of the noise until I saw Mother. She stepped down and gave me a hug and a kiss. When Dad went to kiss her, she turned her face away.

'It's nice to be home,' I heard Mother tell Mrs Wiles the next day. 'After the miscarriage, the convalescence did me good.' Those were big words. Convalescence and miscarriage. What on earth did they mean? How I wished I could go to school then I'd find out. And it would be great to get out of the house more often. Nowadays whenever Dad was home, the atmosphere was charged. He raged because Mother continued to cold-shoulder him.

'It's all your fault!' I could hear her in their bedroom. 'You knew the attic floorboards were rotten. I kept on asking you to repair them. If I hadn't put my foot through and fallen, we might have had a...' The rest was lost in tears.

There were also rows about money. The country markets were no longer providing a living. With better transport facilities villagers were travelling into the city to do their shopping. Dad had opened a shop using borrowed money. It was not going well, which increased the tension. However thrifty Mother was, she could not create meals out of thin air.

There was a diversion for me, however, when the weather was fine. I was allowed a ride in the milkman's cart. I enjoyed every minute as we clip-clopped along, watching Dobbin's tail flick his massive backside. His tail seemed to have a life of its own. On May Day he wore a bonnet with brightly coloured streamers which fluttered in the breeze. At each house Jim lifted me down to watch him ladle milk from his churn into the jugs which stood on the back doorsteps. He never spilled a drop. The jugs were protected from dust and flies by circles of muslin which were weighted down with beads. Sometimes we passed the muffin man with his tray balanced on his head. That tea-time Mother would spike muffins, one by one, on a toasting fork then hold it in front of the fire. They smelled delicious and dripping with butter, tasted even better.

The one outing I detested, even though it included a

tram-car ride, was a visit to the hairdresser's. All the way into town, I promised Mother I wouldn't cry. Once inside Dawson's I was fine, until I felt the clippers' cold steel on the back of my neck. Then I howled, much to Mother's embarrassment.

Despite that, our first visit there after Mother's return to Birmingham from Brighton was memorable. After I had had my hair cut and had stopped caterwauling, I watched Sally wrap Mother in a white cotton smock, then unpin and comb her long, thick, wavy brown hair until it hung down her back. I gazed, fascinated, as Sally started snipping away.

The scissors went further and further up round Mother's head until eventually great clippings of hair like a sheep's fleece lay on the floor. How brave Mother was. She didn't cry when the clippers scraped her neck. The scalping over, what remained of her hair was then shampooed, dried, and combed straight back off her face. 'It's the very latest,' said Sally, holding the mirror up for Mother to see her handiwork. 'It's an Eton Crop.'

Mother seemed very pleased with her new image. She didn't ask me what I thought. Dad said it for me when he came home that night. He entered the room and did a double take. 'Bloody hell!' he shouted as he bent to kiss his wife's frosty cheek. 'It's like kissing a bloody man!' It gave them something different to quarrel about.

Then one day Father did not come home. He had given me no warning and not said goodbye. Mother provided a clue. 'I don't believe in telling children things that might worry them,' she told Mrs Wiles. She was misguided. It was the uncertainty of not knowing which fuelled my imagination, brought on horrible dreams and shattered my nights. Mother did, however, do her best to soothe me in the dark hours when I reached out to clutch her hand. Fortunately I had Bruno, my bear-on-wheels, to play with and my shiny red pedal car. As I drove up and down the street, I pretended I was going to find Dad. My anxiety about him was torture.

Then one morning a letter came for me. I couldn't read it, of course. So I asked yet again, 'When can I go to school?'

'One day,' Mother answered, absentmindedly. I fumed as she read Dad's letter to me. I looked on it as a love-letter for my eyes alone.

'Daddy says Leeds is very nice, but he misses you, and to be a good girl. He sends you his love, and look those are kisses.'

Kisses I could read. Any fool could understand a row of crosses. I could make them myself. I sat down to answer with line after line of scribble, scribble into which I poured my thoughts and feelings. Only the crosses would make sense to Father but he treasured those letters for years.

Where was Leeds, and why had he gone there? Over the weeks that followed snippets of information filtered through to me. Apparently Dad's shop had failed, and he owed a hundred pounds, a frightening debt in 1924. His cousin Nat had offered him a job in his wholesale fur showroom in Leeds, so Dad had gone north, found digs and was paying off his debt before sending Mother the rest of his wages. He was doing his best yet Mother never once spoke of us joining him.

Then one Friday night, Dad came home. He first rushed towards Mother, who as usual turned her face away. 'What a warm welcome! I might just as well not have come home!' Then he hugged me till my ribs cracked. Next morning, there was a gala performance for me in the bathroom, then a romp round Cannon Hill Park.

The stay was short. On Sunday, Dad kissed me goodbye, managed to reach Mother's cheek without a mishap, then went back to Leeds. He had also promised to come home again within a few weeks. At least I now knew he had not abandoned me for good.

Despite my love for my father, I had to admit that life with Mother on her own was peaceful if unexciting. She was much more relaxed and seemed to enjoy grass widowhood. With Dad in Leeds paying off his debt, she now set about cutting expenses in her practical fashion. The dining room furniture and two spare easy chairs were moved upstairs into the best bedroom, and the bedroom suite was moved downstairs into the dining room. A cooker, sink and cupboard were installed in the box room. Presto! We had a furnished flat.

Then the Armands moved in. Even allowing for my loyalty to Dad, not only was life more serene without him, but Marcel Armand was the best bonus I could have had from the upheaval. He was a dark, bonny little boy with kind eyes and, like his mother, only spoke French. His father had come to Birmingham to work for a coach building firm.

Mother and I only spoke English but we all got along splendidly. Mother and Madame Armand kept to their own quarters though we shared the bathroom. Marcel and I played in a state of complete harmony upstairs. I was no longer lonely. I enjoyed Marcel's red engine; he loved my doll's tea-set. We communicated through raised eyebrows, understated mime and intuition. It was a great relationship.

Only once did I come near to disrupting the peace. One morning when I had been called downstairs for my dinner, Mother looked askance at my black hands, knees and clothes.

'Where on earth have you been playing? You're filthy!'

'Under the table in Madame's dining room.'

'Well,' grumbled Mother, 'play somewhere else. She obviously doesn't clean under the table.'

'I haven't to play under your table,' I smiled at Madame

later, 'because Mummy says you don't clean underneath it.'

Madame smiled back at me and patted my head. Fortunately for the Entente Cordiale, she thought I was blithering on about the weather like all the rest of the English.

*

Mother seemed preoccupied of late. She was also getting fatter.

One afternoon I was taken for a walk in the park by the Greenstone's nanny, Edna. She was young but made it obvious she did not want an extra child tagging on to the pram. Once we reached a bench near the lake, she ignored her charge and me, while she gossiped with another nursemaid.

I was bored, standing there, gazing at the murky water as a swan sailed by with its beak in the air. Out of the corner of my eye I realised both girls were looking at me, and whispering. I pricked up my ears.

'Someone's going to have her nose put out of joint, especially if the baby's a girl?' Nanny Greenstone said and they both laughed. I froze.

What was going on at home? Was I being displaced? My stomach churned. Dad would sing *Poor Old Joe* for some new child and Mother would have no time for me at all. So that was why Dr St Johnson had called today and why Mother had stayed in bed. The baby must have been in his black bag. That was where they came from, Mother had said but she had never mentioned she was getting one. Temper and tears were blurring my eyes. My traitorous parents! Yet a real baby would be much nicer to play with than a doll, and I loved my dolls. The baby

11

would be the centre of attention when I got home. I was in a terrible muddle, and could have happily pushed Edna and her friend into the Cannon Hill Park lake.

Back home once again, Nurse Lilley opened the door. She was all navy blue and starched white, a bad-tempered ship in full sail.

'Wipe your feet. Don't make a noise. No, you can't see your Mother. You've had your tea? Now it's hot milk and bed.'

I turned green at the mention of milk. I longed to see Mother and the baby. Where was it? I crept upstairs while Nurse was busy in the kitchen. I paused outside Mother's room. She was sobbing and Father was making comforting noises. Sadness hung like a cloud. That night, without having been allowed to see her, I wept into my pillow for my grieving Mother, the lost baby, and my own dreadful feeling of guilt.

A few days later, Nurse announced that on condition I was well behaved and did nothing to agitate Mother, I could visit her. So I sidled shyly into her room. Mother was leaning back against the white embroidered pillows, wearing her best blue nightie and knitted bed-jacket. Her hair was combed but she looked pale and her eyes were red-rimmed.

She kissed me and tried to smile as I gave her a hug. She smelled of eau-de-Cologne. I would have climbed up for a cuddle but was too scared Nurse would come in.

Auntie Ida was also visiting so I went to stand at the foot of the bed, taking care not to kick the flowered chamberpot underneath. The grown-ups were whispering, their heads together. I tried not to fidget, and looked round at the familiar things; the flowered jug and basin on the grey marble-topped wash stand, the silver-backed comb and brush and matching cut-glass hair-tidy on the mahogany dressing-table. I was just wondering if I could risk playing with an ornate antimony box on the dressing-table, when I heard, 'It was a boy…stillborn..?' Mother was wiping her eyes.

I pushed my head through the wooden panels at the bottom of the bed, hoping to make her smile. She ignored me so I pretended I was a princess, waiting for a prince to rescue me from my castle. When he did not appear, I decided I'd withdraw and play another game. I wriggled. I pulled. I moaned. I was now being a prisoner in the stocks.

Slowly two pairs of eyes turned and focused on me as I struggled to free myself. Mother groaned and collapsed against the pillows while Auntie Ida leapt to my side. To no avail. I could not get my head out again. That was that. They would either have to saw through the bars or cut off my ears. Then Nurse would kill me. She heard the commotion, came running in and took in the situation at a glance. She gave a comforting cluck towards her patient and a ferocious glare at me.

'Keep still, child?' Nurse barked. I was sending up a prayer to the Patron Saint of trapped heads when she reappeared with a jar of vaseline. None too gently she proceeded to lather my head. Then she turned me on my back and eased me out. I had had enough and ran into the bathroom where I hid behind the door. Nurse soon found me and although it wasn't even Friday, gave me a bath and a shampoo.

That night I had an attack of croup, when I wheezed and gasped for breath. It was the first of many and the treatment was simple. The steam kettle boiled all night on an electric radiator, my chest was anointed with eucalyptus oil and Dr St Johnson was sent for. He came puffing up the stairs to prescribe a remedy so awful it cured me of enjoying the fuss.

I had to drink a mug of boiled milk containing bicarbonate of soda. Swallowing the skin on the milk was worse than enduring an attack.

A spate of sore throats followed, which threw Mother into a panic as there had been an epidemic of diphtheria that year and many children had died. In between ailments, I asked repeatedly to go to school.

'You aren't five yet, then we'll see.' Mother was too busy pumping Virol in to me to listen. I was certain that at four-and-a half, I was ready for anything. But not my next excursion.

I was taken to a strange large house and left alone in a downstairs bedroom with Bonzo for company. At a recent visit to *Aladdin And His Lamp*, Widow Twankey had thrown soft toys into the audience and I had caught Bonzo.

It was nearly lunchtime and the smell of cooking was making me feel hungry. A woman in a white coat put her head round the door, 'There's no lunch for you, young lady. You're going to the theatre this afternoon?' I was puzzled. I loved the theatre; was Mother going to take me to see *Cinderella*, and if so, where was she? Before I could say Ugly Sister, I was carried upstairs into a room full of huge lights, stainless steel vats, equipment and a sickly smell. Two men in white coats and masks pinioned me down on to a table and, as I was convinced they were going to murder me, I put up a violent struggle. There I'd been dreaming of the panto. I'd never trust Mother again. A chloroform pad was held over my face.

I gave Mother hell when I was allowed home and refused to eat. For one thing my throat was too sore now I was minus my tonsils.

Also I was lonely, recuperating upstairs on my own. The Armands had long since gone back to France. Dad was still working in Leeds but had paid off his debt, so we now had a maid called Hilda. She took a savage delight in pinching me whenever Mother was out. My nightmares increased. I dreamt I was being held down by Hilda and two giants, intent on cutting my throat. Early one morning, feeling isolated and bored, I sat up in bed looking at my comic. I longed to be able to read it. I couldn't, so I made two elephant's tusks out of rolled-up bits of Tiger Tim and wedged them up my nose. Just as I was imagining I was crashing round the jungle I drew a deep breath and inhaled one of the tusks.

At that moment Mother came round the door, and her look of surprise turned to horror when I confessed I had lost one tusk already down the back of my nose. She didn't hesitate. I was bundled round to Dr St Johnson who was still in his dressing-gown. 'Not you again?' he said, throwing me a baleful look over his glasses followed by a probing with long forceps. 'A fraction further and you'd have choked' put me off playing that game again.

The tedium of my convalescence was relieved by a wonderful new toy Dad had brought home: a crystal set. I was fascinated, twiddling the cat's whisker until music came down the earphones. I thought it magic and could have listened all day. Unfortunately my increased nightmares were blamed on the set and it was banned. I was frustrated and angry.

Eventually I was allowed downstairs again. Mother was out for the afternoon and Hilda was in front of the fire, cutting her hair. Bits of her fringe sizzled in the flames and smelled of brilliantine. Then she left the room, savagely pinching my legs as she went. I picked up the scissors and, feeling for a lump of my fringe, sliced it off. I leaned over the fireguard and in a moment my hair was sizzling, too. I was disappointed there was no smell of brilliantine. Cutting was such fun I foraged in Mother's work basket and found her latest piece of knitting. There was always some work in hand. Mother knitted all my clothes; dresses, combinations and hateful socks which made ridges in my feet and were too thick for my shoes. As in a dream I picked up some half-finished combs and cut a neat square out of one sleeve. Then I put it back in the basket.

When Mother came home wearing her best navy dress, she looked plump and pretty, despite her cropped hair. She was smiling as she bent to kiss me until she noticed my fringe. 'What have you done?' Mother's mouth was gaping.

'Hilda did it!' I cried. 'She cut her own hair, then mine!'

Mother shook her head in disbelief and called Hilda to come downstairs. While she waited, she picked up her knitting. When she saw the sleeve matched my fringe, she stood up, her mouth tight from annoyance and I braced myself for punishment. This was going to involve a smacked bottom unless I was mistaken. But I had a lot to learn about grown-ups.

Mother had forgotten the whopper I had told, she was so angry with Hilda for leaving scissors around for me to use. When Hilda appeared, she received the full blast of Mother's wrath instead of me!

'And she nips me!' I managed to blurt out. Hilda shot me such a malevolent glare that I backed into the corner of the room. That did it. Mother believed me.

'You can pack your bags and go!' Mother said, out-glaring Hilda. It had certainly been an eventful afternoon. My only regret was that I had not found any socks to cut while I was at it.

*

When Mother was putting me to bed she often told me stories about her family. She was proud that her ancestors had settled in Britain several generations ago yet were as orthodox as any rabbi. Who had told her only to cut nails alternately, and never on Fridays, I didn't ask. But according to Mother, only corpses had their nails cut one after the other. Also she always said 'K.N.' after anything was praised. 'It's short for kineahora,' Mother said, 'a spell to ward off the evil eye.'

Mother's mother, who died before I was born, was the eldest of twelve children and had endured years of pram-pushing, with the next in line sitting on the baby's toes and a toddler hanging on to the handle. Not surprisingly, after Grandma married, she only had three children: Eva, Mother, and Natalie.

Mother's grandmother had had a struggle feeding twelve mouths and therefore developed economy to a fine art. She marked the milk jug at night in case anyone was tempted to sneak down for a drink in the small hours. Every meat meal was preceded by a large helping of potato kugel and gravy to dull the appetite before the joint was carved. Even in their more prosperous years, Grandmother Samuels still only served half a kipper per person for a meal. But frugal ways were relaxed when their Golden Wedding came round. They celebrated it in great style with a slap-up eight course dinner catered in a hall.

A Golden Wedding was such a rarity in 1902 that it attracted much attention. A crowd of sightseers in their everyday clothes waited outside to see the carriages arrive with the guests in their evening gowns and jewellery. 'It was a gala event,' Mother recalled. 'Even the Lord Mayor attended.' I was sorry it was before my time, although I should not have fancied the entree. It was stewed pigeon.

All Mother's aunts and uncles were there: Auntie Rae, who sported a ginger wig and guarded her true age like a state secret, and also Uncle Manny who owned a skating rink and was an enthusiastic inventor. His biggest success was a machine for issuing metal tokens at cinema box offices.

The family gossip was always interesting: Manny did not speak to his brother Lewin, also a confirmed bachelor, although no-one could remember what they had quarrelled about. They were both dapper, nice looking men with great drive and business ability. Once I had overheard Mother telling Auntie Eva, 'Uncle Manny has a lady living with him, who's supposed to be his housekeeper!' Why they laughed at this, I didn't know. Uncle Lewin, so their tongues wagged, also had a married lady friend in the background. Mother had no idea then that both uncles would eventually leave most of their money to their many nieces and nephews, much to her delight!

Uncle Lewin was very popular with Mother and me because he had recently acquired the Futurist Cinema in John Bright Street. A cafe upstairs opened on to a balcony, which provided the most marvellous vantage point for watching the yearly Rag procession, or anything else of note which was going on below.

On one occasion, I was taken to gaze down on a large open car driving slowly along. In the back sat a young man in a sombre black overcoat. The light reflected on his golden hair, a brighter colour than I had ever seen. He looked lonely as he gravely acknowledged the crowds. 'That's the Prince of Wales,' Mother said, as we joined in the cheering. 'He'll be King one day.'

Mother loved going to Uncle Lewin's cinema, and we went often as she was admitted for nothing. Lillian Gish, Ronald Colman, Ramon Navarro and Douglas Fairbanks all wove their spell. For myself I preferred Felix the Cat and I was bored with the grown-ups' films, all the rolling eyes and kissing. Words came on to the screen every few minutes and frustrated me even more because I couldn't read them. 'When can I go to school?' I tugged Mother's sleeve.

'One day,' Mother said, and sighed. She was more interested in Rudolph Valentino than what I was saying. He was certainly different from my dad, although Dad must have caused Mother's romantic heart to flutter when he was courting her. He hadn't arrived on a white horse but had roared up Hagley Road on a motor bike. The local rabbi had arranged the match when Mother was in her late twenties.

He had assured her father that Dad, although four years younger than Mother and from a poor East End home, was hard-working and respectable. He had not discovered that Dad was also volatile, noisy and had a terrible temper.

Mother, on the other hand, was a pretty, refined woman, living with her quiet studious father who was by now a widower. This gave her little experience in dealing with an excitable man like Dad. Mother was attracted by his lively manner. Also he spoke well with no trace of a cockney accent. He, in turn, was impressed by her father's standing in the Birmingham community. Dad soon proposed and a year later they were married.

There was trouble from the start. Dad's expectations as to a dowry were soon dashed. Grandpa had already put his hand in his pocket for one son-in-law who had turned out to be work-shy so he was not prepared to stake another.

Dad was certainly not afraid of hard work. He was making a living selling in outlying markets. Tall and good looking, with dark curly hair combed back from fleshy features, he also had a good voice, a gift for mimicry, a ready wit and a string of jokes culled from the music halls. He had no difficulty in drawing a crowd. The punters loved him, even when the lace curtaining — 'Finest quality, contains no starch or dressing whatever' — was moved from where it had been draped over his shoulder to reveal a layer of dressing as thick as a burst bag of icing sugar. They laughed even more on one icy morning when Dad was selling rolls of congoleum, a cheap form of lino. 'This lino is magnificent value — it's indestructible — will wear forever!' he boomed. With this he gave the frost-bitten roll an approving smack and it shattered into smithereens. But he was never chased by anyone, for as he said to Mother, 'Everything I touch is kosher.' She sniffed back. 'But not that army-condemned tinned salmon you sold at Banbury!'

Dad not only entertained his customers, he kept me happy whenever he was at home. The bathroom ceiling shook to *On with the motley, the paint and the powder!* as Dad scraped his blue jowls with a wicked cut-throat razor. I could expect a splosh of shaving soap on my nose which stung my eyes but I didn't mind. It was all part of the fun as he lifted his nose out of the way, negotiating round his top lip and the high notes. In the best traditions of grand opera he finished up spilling blood but, in his case, through bits of cotton wool. After *Rigoletto* came *Poor Old Joe*, my favourite spiritual, then the *Song Of The Flea*. This usually made Dad cough more than he sang. For an encore he acted out *Little Red Riding Hood*, followed by *The Three Little Pigs*. He would ham it up with popping eyes and hair on end, slicing the air with his razor.

Mother could have Valentino. I missed my dad.

*

I must have asked once too often, 'When can I go to school?' because one morning I was dressed in my best heather mixture knitted dress with the white rabbit wool edging. I still couldn't tie my shoelaces myself but decided not to make a fuss or complain about my thick, hand-knitted socks. I didn't want to make Mother change her mind. The big day had arrived. I was going to enrol at Mrs Levy's kindergarten.

I held Mother's hand tightly as I skipped through Cannon Hill Park. I was not used to being taken out before nine in the morning and the park was deserted.

The only occupants were the ducks and swans on the lake. There was an autumnal haze in the air which masked an orange sun. Eventually we arrived at an Edwardian terraced house, where a formidable looking Mrs Levy met us.

Suddenly I was terrified. What had I done? Why had I nagged to go to school? Would I like it and more important, would Mother come back for me at dinner time? It was too late now to change my mind, even to annoy Mother. I was inside and had my coat taken off.

The school room had tall sash windows on the left and Mrs Levy's desk ahead. At her side, a large blackboard on an easel was covered with coloured chalk drawings illustrating the alphabet. There were twenty children sitting in pairs at low desks. I was to share with Rose, who wore a blue velvet dress with a white lace collar. I noted with chagrin that no-one else wore a knitted dress. Mrs Levy's remark, 'And did your mother make your beautiful dress?' only mollified me slightly.

The lesson started with Mrs Levy pointing to the blackboard; her stick rested on the red apple.

'What is A for?'

Rose put her hand up. 'A is for Apple.'

This was going to be a doddle.

'And what does B stand for?'

The answer was so easy I nearly leapt out of my seat.

'B is for suitcase.'

I was appalled at the shrieks of laughter which filled the air. If the silly woman wanted B to stand for bag, why had she drawn a suitcase? I might have exploded with rage and been expelled on my first day, had not Brenda, a lovely little blonde child in front of me, laughed so much that she made a puddle in her chair. That at least took the attention away from me. Later, there was some more excitement. A boom of guns could be heard in the distance.

'We will be silent for a moment, children,' Mrs Levy explained. 'Queen Alexandra has died.'

The morning passed quickly. Rose and I licked each other's tongues behind Mrs Levy's back and pulled faces at the taste; an experiment we did not repeat. At break everyone ate biscuits or fruit. Mother had given me an apple but I was too keyed up to manage more than one bite, and hid the remainder under my dress until it fell out and rolled on to the floor, ending up in the waste basket. I expected to be punished for not eating it all but nothing happened. When Mrs Levy had left us alone for a minute, Michael jumped on to a chair and declaimed at the top of his voice. I was very impressed. Then it was time to go home.

I need not have worried that Mother would abandon me for she was on the school step, waiting.

'What have you learnt today?' she asked fondly, when we arrived home. I jumped on to a chair, waved a ruler in the air and shouted Michael's battle-cry, 'I'm the king of the castle and you're a dirty old rascal!'

Mother looked aghast, in fact, quite displeased. I thought it was great, the best part of the morning. That is apart from Brenda's little accident.

The days went by with their own rhythm. The mornings were spent at Mrs Levy's where I learnt the alphabet but not how to put the letters together. Words were still a meaningless jumble.

One morning there was great excitement when I came out of school. A father had called to collect his daughter in a big motorcar, wonder of wonders. He kindly offered Mother and me a lift home. I had never been in a car before. It was an open tourer so Mother anxiously buttoned my coat high into my neck and pulled my hat down over my ears. The upholstery was of brown leather, the dashboard fittings were silver and there was a carnation in a vase. Mother and I felt like royalty.

Dad came home that night. I hid under the bedclothes as the walls shook.

'I've had two years on my own in digs and I'm not standing for it any longer. Either you give notice and pack up and join me, or else...' His voice dropped to a mumble so I couldn't hear what the threat entailed but it would mean trouble, that much I could tell.

'I don't want to leave here, I won't know anyone.' Mother was sobbing her heart out.

'It's up to you.' Dad thumped the table to emphasise each word, then slammed the door and stormed up to bed.

The next morning Mother's eyes were puffy and sore. 'We're going to live in Leeds,' she said with a shudder. I was delighted. I'd be with Dad again and going to Leeds would be an adventure.

During the next few weeks, Mother's lack of enthusiasm for the prospective move never altered but packing cases were filled, pictures came down from the walls and the silver and china were packed in layers of paper. She was as unhappy as if she had suffered a bereavement and sometimes lay in bed, prostrate from crying.

The last two weeks were spent in our best clothes, going round saying goodbye. Our first trip was to London to see Dad's Mother.

'Goodness knows when we'll be able to afford to come down here again,' Mother sighed as the train drew into Paddington. She loved the atmosphere of the big city and I was so excited I felt sick.

We caught a taxi-cab and Mother told him to drive us round Piccadilly, so that I could see Eros and the flower girls. The West End was a kaleidoscope of coloured lights, flashing signs advertising theatres, huge, brightly lit shop windows, and very tall, elegantly dressed people. Soon we left the bright lights behind and before long we approached the narrower streets of Dalston. That was where Grandma lived with Uncle Aaron, Auntie Rose and their family. Their house was old with three storeys as well as a basement. Uncle and Aunt lived below stairs; the middle floors were let and Grandma had two rooms in the attic. Her rooms were large and light and she kept them spotless.

We panted up the three flights of stairs, and there was Grandma hugging me tight. She was a small, slight, quiet lady, with white hair which made her look very frail but nevertheless she must have been much tougher than she looked, to have survived without a husband to support her. Fortunately, she could sew and had done some tailoring, which combined with buying a bit of this and that for re-sale, had kept the wolf from baying too near the door. It had been a struggle and she had never had a holiday.

We sat down for lunch at the big kitchen table covered by a cross-stitched linen cloth. The minced-meat pancakes made my mouth water and so did the 'stuffed monkeys', fruit-filled pastries which Mother loved but had never asked Grandma how to make.

Much to my delight Uncle Aaron and his two sons, Geoff and Sammy, came upstairs to join us for tea. It was the first time I had seen Geoff since he had come to live with us, after Uncle Aaron had turned up unexpectedly with him from London. Uncle Aaron had said to Dad, 'Do me a favour, Joe, and find him a job. There won't be so many distractions in Birmingham.' Uncle Aaron was eleven years older than Dad and had helped bring Dad up ever since their father had deserted them. Geoff was tall, fair, handsome and easygoing. Although he was eighteen when he moved in with us, he didn't mind playing with a three-year-old and made a big fuss of me. I adored him nearly as much as I did Dad. Geoff had especially come in handy for winding up the gramophone. It stood in a handsome oak cabinet with a big horn attached, in the front room window.

I loved listening to *In a love nest, cosy and warm* which I thought referred to birds but my favourite was Lottie Collins singing songs from *The Maid of the Mountains.*

Everyone was impressed with the fact that although I could not read, I could identify the records. Yet it was easy, I just recognised the shape of the words in the titles.

Dad had found Geoff a job, and kept him for nothing to get him started, but soon found that Geoff was more enthusiastic about winding the gramophone than he was about work. Dad had to dig him out of bed most mornings.

Finally, after several months when they were feeling the pinch, Dad broached the question of Geoff's board. Geoff laughed it off. His shoes needed repairing, he needed a new suit, next month would be easier. He had several cast-iron excuses as to why he couldn't contribute anything towards his keep.

On Mother's birthday, Dad took her to see George Robey at the Hippodrome. They panted up three flights of carpeted stairs, then the stone steps to the balcony. It was all Dad could afford but he had managed a small box of chocolates for Mother. When the lights went up for the interval, Mother was just about to start on the chocolates when Dad nudged her. His face was thunderous as he pointed to a distant but easily recognisable figure in the front stalls, his right arm round a flashy blonde, his left hand clutching a fat cigar. It was Geoff.

'That does it,' said Dad, settling back on the wooden form to enjoy the rest of the show in discomfort. Later that night, Dad roared his displeasure to his nephew. It was a toss-up which had annoyed him more, Geoff's taste in expensive theatre seats or girls. The next day Geoff was sent back to Uncle Aaron.

Sitting at the table I wondered how Geoff and Mother

would get on now. He smiled a bit sheepishly and Mother gave him a frosty look but made no reference to the escapade.

Uncle Aaron, Geoff and Sammy had exactly the same volatile personality as my father and were soon happily thumping the table and shouting about nothing in particular. Since there was no malice in the raised voices I did not feel threatened.

The sunlight from the dormer window shone on Grandma's white hair and the pink and gold decorated plates displayed on the dresser. Grandma was smiling, busy at the cooker, enjoying her family. I felt sleepy and very happy. Mother had forgotten for the moment that she would soon be moving into the wilderness.

That evening, I was put to bed in an armchair which had an extension pulled out. Next to me was Grandma's high double brass bed, with its two thick feather perronies and huge pillows she had brought from Russia. She was going to share with Mother. Cousins Jeanette and Marion shared a double bed at the other end of the room. While Mother was out at the theatre and before the girls had come to bed, Grandma and I were both tucked up in our beds. We started to talk to each other, asking questions, sharing secrets.

Grandma told me how she had hidden in her home town in Russia when the Cossacks had scythed along the streets, killing any Jew in their path. Her English was good and her Russian accent added a piquancy to the conversation. She asked me what I liked doing and I told her all about the kindèrgarten and how I was looking forward to going to a proper school. I didn't tell her about the rows or anything unpleasant.

It was the most rewarding experience. For the first time in my life an adult talked to me as if I were much older than five, and actually listened to what I was saying. I fell asleep finally, exhausted but content.

When I awoke in the morning, Mother was still asleep but Grandma was already busy in the kitchen. I sat up in my makeshift bed, then climbed out and into the hollow Grandma had left in hers. Snuggling in the feather bed was like floating on warm clouds. It was bliss compared with a mattress.

There was much yawning from the other end of the room as my cousins came to. Much older than me, they at first amused themselves by teasing me but soon relented and invited me to join them in their bed. My mouth dropped when I realised both girls had gone to bed fully dressed, apart from their cardigans and shoes. I wondered what Mother would make of that. Then the girls taught me the only athletic manoeuvre I was ever to accomplish: to turn a somersault on their bed.

There was no bathroom, only a sink in a cupboard on the downstairs landing. 'Make sure you have a good wash,' Marion called out as she raced past without stopping for a lick and a promise herself. That was a bit of a cheek I thought!

We had breakfast with Grandma. Before we left, she gave Mother a bag of her homemade biscuits and a large parcel for me.

'These are some things for you,' she touched my cheek. 'I won't see you grow up, so I want you to have something useful, for when you are married.' There were silver candlesticks, two elaborate Madeira-worked table cloths and a silver dish for a bread board. Although I appreciated the presents were beautiful, such a thing as getting married seemed to me then as remote as a trip to the moon. I'd much rather have had a doll's pram. However, I had the grace to be ashamed of myself and thanked her with a hug and a kiss. I loved her very much. I couldn't guess how much I should treasure the gifts when I was older.

We kissed her goodbye and went down into the

basement, where the rest of the family lived. The view through their living-room window was of disembodied ankles and feet walking along the pavement and it was impossible to see the sky. Inside, the room was gloomy, which was an advantage, as there was a layer of dust over the furniture. Aunt was dressed but her hair was not combed. The three men came out of the bedrooms with their braces dangling over crumpled trousers, their hair dishevelled. All, it seemed, slept in their clothes!

'Rose is a slut,' Mother sniffed on the train going home. 'Always has been, so the rest of them know no better.' Thus she dismissed Aunt from the conversation with a second, even more contemptuous sniff.

What Mother had not noticed was that all the family seemed devoted to their mother, and whenever Uncle Aaron went to kiss her, she held up her face with a smile. I thought it a pity that the two sisters-in-law could not have been shaken up in a bag together.

I asked Mother about the big picture on Uncle's living room wall. It was a sepia-tinted photograph of a handsome man with a broad beard. Uncle Aaron, although clean shaven, looked his double.

'That was your grandfather,' Mother's voice was low, 'and don't ever mention him to your father as it upsets him'.

Fleeing from the pogroms when Dad was a baby, Grandpa had gone on to America to seek his fortune, leaving Grandma in London to fend for herself and their sons. In the end it was clear that Grandfather had forgotten to send for them. He never sent a penny maintenance, any word of explanation or enquiry as to their welfare. Finally Grandma had obtained a *Get*, a divorce, and was well rid of him.

I seethed that he should have treated them so badly; my dad and lovely, gentle Gran. How different Dad might have been with a father to look up to. It was to be many years before that chapter was closed, and even then, the resentment festered on.

Grandfather had married twice more in America and had more children; but when he was very old and, it seemed, hard up, he wrote to Aaron asking if he could have some support from his almost forgotten sons. Grandpa certainly had plenty of chutzpa. Dad, usually a soft touch, didn't take long to make up his mind.

'Tell him to go to Hell!' he said.

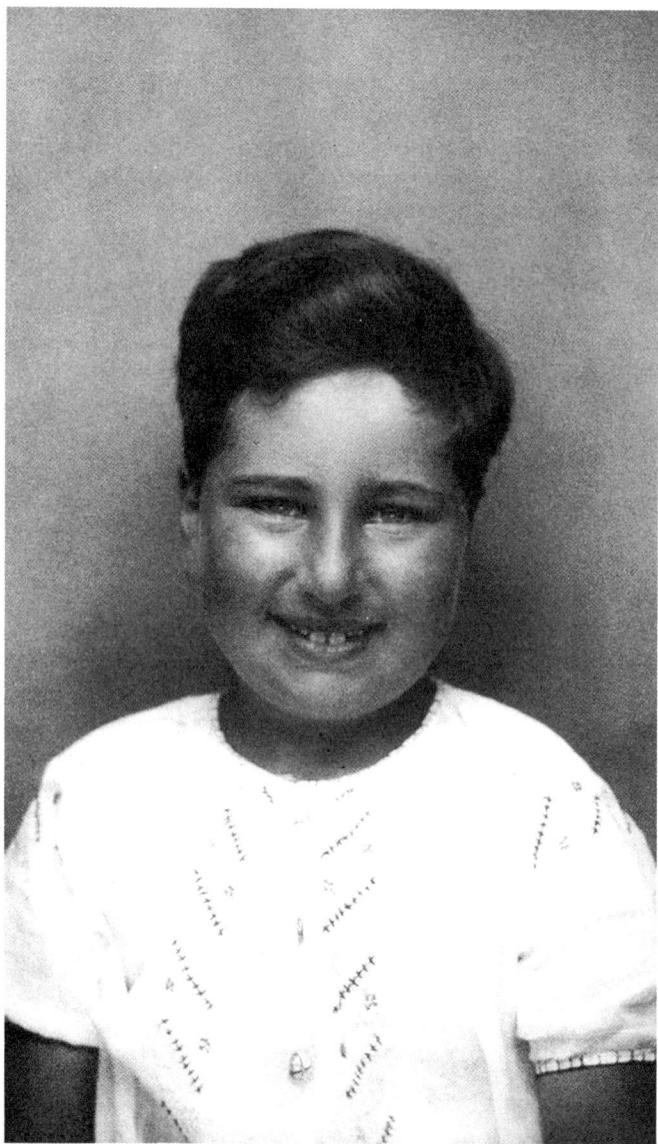

Chapter Two

Before we migrated north we were obliged to call and pay our respects to Grandpa and Laura, his second wife, and I was not looking forward to it. Grandpa was a forbidding figure. It was not that he was particularly tall, just stern. There was neither a cuddle nor a bristly kiss from him, let alone an affectionate pinch of my cheeks. Yet despite being such a cold fish he and Grandma had been happy together. He had fled from Poland when he was seventeen, become fluent in English, then gone into business as a pawnbroker. Yet his first love was studying the Talmud.

He and Grandmother had begun married life over the shop; then when they prospered, had moved into his present house. We were never there long enough for me to gain much impression of it, other than it was large, with a beautiful garden. Mother knew it well and had many happy memories of her years there, when her mother was alive.

Laura had first been Grandpa's housekeeper, but after six months had threatened to leave if her position were not upgraded. Grandpa had had so much trouble finding an orthodox housekeeper that he had agreed to marry her. They seemed compatible but there was no love lost between Laura and her step-daughters. Natalie, the youngest, and the only one still living at home when her father had re-married, soon left and was now living in Paris. Laura had refused to entertain any of the family at any time, not even on the Holy days. Instead, she and Grandpa stayed in a kosher hotel whenever work threatened. She certainly ruled the roost, as Grandpa would not have dreamed of spending Passover anywhere but at home before Laura's arrival. Grandma, with

Mother's help, had regularly catered for as many as forty for a Seder. 'It was all right for my poor mother to slave her guts out, but not the second one,' Mother said.

'I trust Joan's Hebrew education is not being neglected?' Grandpa said to Mother.

'All in good time,' she muttered, which roughly translated meant: 'Over my dead body!' Her attitude was understandable. Grandpa had roused her at six-thirty every day during her childhood to teach her Hebrew. She still bore a grudge.

We were not pressed to stay. Grandpa did not seem to notice or mind that Laura had not offered us so much as a cup of tea. The air outside was less chilly but Mother's eyes were sad and tears trickled down her cheeks as we walked home.

Visiting Auntie Eva and her children, Vera, Dorothy, Mirrie, Victor and Beryl was much more enjoyable. Eva, ten years older than Mother, was small, slim, and birdlike. She and Mother had never been close because of the age gap. When we arrived, we followed Aunt Eva down the dark passage into the kitchen, where a narrow window gave little light. A fire blazed in the black-leaded range, cheering up the room and drying a steaming bunting of handkerchiefs strung across the mantelpiece. Some were also draped over the fireguard.

Beryl, the youngest, had a streaming cold and as fast as she soaked a hanky, it was hung up to dry without having first been washed. Mother's eyes gleamed disapproval. Poor Beryl! She was the youngest and had inherited one of my cast-off knitted dresses, from which some of the stitches had parted company at the shoulder seam. They were unravelling before our eyes. A repair was needed that Mother could have done standing on her head but Aunt Eva had not bothered. She was happier with more intellectual pursuits than mending. Dorothy had inherited her intellect, so was known as the 'clever one'. She was a thin, pretty, fair girl, with an ethereal pallor so she was also labelled 'delicate', which led me to believe that frailty went with brilliance. Dorothy and Vera were both much older than I and way past childish games. Victor escaped upstairs as he was shy but Mirrie, who was nearer my age, was prepared to play with me.

Mother and Aunt Eva chatted away while Beryl sneezed and Mirrie and I played Snakes and Ladders. Dorothy had her nose in a book. I wondered if some of her brains, already used successfully for a scholarship, would rub off on me. Mother glanced from Dorothy to me, as if she were hoping along the same lines. But with my plump arms and legs, I couldn't have looked delicate if I had tried. Mother and Aunt Eva were looking at a newspaper cutting which Mother had found when she was packing. It was a report of Aunt Eva's wedding in 1907. I knew Mother had been hurt that she had not been chosen to be a bridesmaid because she was taller than the bride. The photograph showed Uncle Sam in such a high, stiff collar it amazed me he could breathe, let alone smile. Aunt Eva, with her hair piled high, looked beautiful in an elaborate dress of 'charmeuse, trimmed with orange blossom, and wearing a pearl necklace.' A ribbon by ribbon account of the dresses followed and there was a full description of the wedding gifts, including a 'tea-cosy from the maid.' The reverse of the cutting gave an account of a young man's attempted suicide by gunshot in a railway carriage. His farewell letter said his head had been turned by his young lady's frolicsomeness. Fortunately he was a rotten shot and had recovered.

'But what's frolicsomeness, Mother?' I asked. 'Never you mind,' Mother said — her usual answer when the conversation grew interesting.

Laura and her likeness to Cinderella's stepmother was the next topic, then our forthcoming move. Dorothy's remarkable prowess at school was praised, and the children's terrible chilblains were lamented. Then we had lunch.

How I envied my cousins. They had each other for company, and the most delicious fish and parsley sauce, like my mother never made. They appeared to live in a peaceful household and were all attending a good school.

Years later, my cousins enlightened me. I couldn't have been more wrong. Their mother never made such a good meal again and Dorothy's 'delicacy' was eventually diagnosed as malnutrition. What was more, Eva and Sam were so badly matched that their rows outdid my parents'. As for their grammar school education, only one scholarship helped out and they were regularly embarrassed at school by threats to send them home if their fees were not paid forthwith. On top of that the girls also confessed to a life-long envy of my knitted dresses; and of my thick, ribbed, woollen socks, especially suitable for their chilblains.

That evening, Mother's face was red and puffy as she tucked me up. I wondered if she would ever look happy again but she managed to smile the next day as we rattled along, sitting on the top deck of a tram, enjoying the sunny breeze and the view of the world below. Mother's favourite Uncle Joe and Auntie Gertie lived in West Bromwich and we were going to say goodbye.

I felt awestruck as usual when we approached their house. The circular drive and marble pillars at either side of the front door were imposing. Our terraced house only sported a bit of privet in the front. Auntie Gertie was at the door to greet us. She was as lovely as the picture-postcard beauties, with dark wavy hair, regular features and large, warm brown eyes. It was easy to see why Uncle had fallen for her despite the difficulties it had presented. Auntie Gertie had been baptised C. of E. She had, however, decided to convert to Judaism, and had moved in with Mother's parents for instruction. This was a difficult task which involved learning Hebrew and the Kashrut laws but a year later she passed the conversion exam. In that time Aunt and Mother had grown fond of each other. Aunt Gertie was always very kind to us.

We were ushered into the dining room where French windows opened on to a huge lawn, the centrepiece of which was an elegant pink marble bird-bath, mounted on stone slabs. 'It's only just arrived from Italy,' Uncle Joe said. He was a keen gardener and proud of the flower beds.

Their dining room was ruled by a parrot which sat in the corner on the perch inside his cage, preening his brilliant red and blue plumage. Every so often, he looked up and cast a bad tempered eye over the Jacobean furniture, Turkey patterned carpet, and us, no doubt fancying a couple of fingers for lunch. Uncle Joe warned me to keep a safe distance as his parrot could bite to the bone.

Uncle Joe was also intimidating. He once tore a strip off Mother for daring to poke his dining-room fire. 'Very bad manners!' he had snapped. Mother said he adored children. He may have done but he terrified me with his sharp line in sarcasm. I was relieved that today, his younger daughter, who was away at boarding school, was the butt of his humour. She had written home describing how she had spent some time swinging in a 'hamuck.'

Tired of sitting still, I asked permission to go and explore. I wandered round the elegant drawing room next door. On top of the grand piano beside the holiday snapshots of the family cruising to the Canary Islands, stood a Spanish doll in frilled skirt, mantilla, and dangling earrings. I picked her up, then put her back as if I had been stung. She was hiding a telephone under her skirt. I had never been near one before and should have run a mile rather than answer it. From there I passed through the conservatory, with its cane furniture and tinkling glass mobile, into the garden. I crunched along the gravel path behind a hedge towards the vegetables but found nothing there to play with, only cabbages in military rows. I skipped back to the lawn, looking in vain for a daisy or two, and ended up dancing round the bird bath. Round and round I whirled, singing *Here we go round the mulberry bush* until I grew giddy, lost my balance and clutched wildly at the base of the bird bath.

Too late, I discovered that the bowl was a separate entity with a life of its own. It flew off the column, blocked the sun from my eyes and only missed my head by a fraction before crashing down on to the flags below. Neither all the King's horses nor anyone else would be able to mend it. Not only was my head still spinning but my stomach was now churning to match. I looked up from the devastation towards the dining room window, where three pairs of eyes were boring through me. I walked across the lawn taking as long as possible.

With commendable control, Uncle Joe barked, 'With the entire garden to play in, did you have to play round the bird bath?'

'Uncle imported it from Italy,' Aunt Gertie added with a sigh which conveyed her reproach. Whether from shock or idiocy I don't know, but my first reaction was to mutter under my breath. 'What a fuss over a mouldy old bird bath! It could have killed me!'

Mother looked as if she might finish off what the bird bath had started. Fortunately I soon came to my senses and apologised. Uncle Joe and Aunt Gertie were marvellous and never mentioned it again.

When Aunt Gertie wanted the table cleared, the maid appeared as if by magic; there was a bell under the table top. At home our bell was on the wall but it registered on the same kind of panel in the kitchen.

Lunch was a treat. We had creamed corn on toast, a

recipe discovered on their travels; then a roast and all the trimmings, followed by jam roly-poly. I was told to leave a little something on the plate, 'For Miss Manners,' Aunt Gertie said. I forgot and ate everything up with gusto, which made Uncle Joe laugh. I relaxed. I was forgiven.

When it was time to go, Uncle Joe gave me half-a-crown which under the circumstances was generous of him but then I might have ended up in hospital having my nails cut in a straight line. I shivered.

'Are you cold?' Mother said.

'No,' I replied, 'just goosy.'

I must admit I was glad to leave the grandeur behind and get home to the packing cases. The lecture I was expecting from Mother while she was putting me to bed did not materialise. As we were leaving the next day, I slept with her. That night whenever I awoke, I could hear her sobbing. I patted her arm.

For me, the prospect of seeing Dad again was more exciting than Christmas Eve. I could not understand why Mother didn't share my enthusiasm.

*

The next day Mother woke me early as the removal men were due at eight o'clock.

'Do hurry up. Wash your hands and face and then go down for your breakfast.' With that she disappeared to let Mrs Wiles in.

I wandered over to the window to have a last look at my favourite tree. I'd played underneath it with real and imaginary friends many a time. Now a squirrel was leaping down the trunk. I watched, fascinated, and only half heard Mother call up from the kitchen, 'Have you done as I told you?'

What had she told me to do? I answered 'Yes!' just to be on the safe side then dragged myself away from the window and pulled on my vest, liberty bodice, knickers and socks. The dress took a bit longer, then my shoes. I could tie my own laces now.

'Do hurry up!' Mother's anxious voice had me running to the top of the stairs where I slowed down before reaching the treacherous bend. In the hall, Bonzo was sitting on top of a packing case. There were patches on the wallpaper where the pictures had been. The house looked shabby, impersonal; waiting to be rid of us. I ate my boiled egg and soldiers in silence. Today there was no need for Mother to post each spoonful into my mouth with 'This is a letter to Daddy'. Suddenly I felt strange. I was going to another town, another house.

As I sat there I was tempted for a second to rock my chair and tip myself backwards just to delay things but concussion didn't seem such a good idea with most of our home already dismantled. While I ate, I watched Mrs Wiles cleaning out the grate. The coconut matting was already rolled up and labelled. The fireguard was in the hall along with a trunk, cases, bucket, clothes horse, a collection of saucepans, meat dishes, trays, and my doll's pram. The men were already loading the van when Mother went upstairs. Suddenly there was a shriek from the bathroom. I rushed up to her and found her packing the toilet things and waving my flannel aloft. 'It's bone dry! How dare you tell me such a whopper! You haven't washed yourself at all!'

So that's what I'd been told to do! While Mother gave me a lick-and-a-promise she lectured me on the wickedness of telling lies. 'And liars need good memories,' Mother added. This mystified me. I was glad I'd avoided a smack. I'd only once felt her hand and that was for disappearing into a neighbour's and being 'lost' for an hour. Once, in a tantrum, I'd put my tongue out at

Mother and been so smartly chucked under the chin it nearly cost me half my tongue. I never tried it again.

Soon we had our hats and coats on and said goodbye to Mrs Wiles, who was going to lock up and leave the key with the landlord. I looked round but could not see Bruin-on-wheels or my beloved motor car. They must have had a packing case all to themselves. I decided not to natter, having only just climbed out of hot water.

In the taxi on our way to New Street station we passed the baker's. I felt a pang at leaving Kunzle's cakes behind but soon I'd see Dad again. Excitement was taking over.

We had the railway compartment to ourselves. The whistle was blown, the green flag waved and we were off. Soon the Birmingham chimneys were left behind. There was a picture of a seaside above Mother's head but I only had eyes for the view through the window: green fields and cows lazily munching. Mother seemed more relaxed now we were on our way. There was some activity in the next compartment as 'Tickets please!' echoed along the corridor.

'Quick!' Mother hissed, 'lie down on that seat opposite, shut your eyes and don't say a word!' I was too flabbergasted to argue so did as I was told. Mother just had time to cover me up with my coat before the inspector appeared.

I could hear him punching Mother's ticket.

'Have you a ticket for the child?'

I froze. I knew he must be looking at me.

'Oh, she's under age,' said Mother firmly.

'How old is she?' He sounded suspicious.

Mother replied in a la-di-da voice, and with such conviction she sounded like a duchess with her hand on the bible. 'She's three,' she said. I smothered a gasp. The inspector must have been satisfied because he left. Had my legs uncurled from under the coat, I should have been revealed as the biggest three year-old outside a circus. I felt as humiliated as if I'd been made to suck a dummy. The farce was repeated three times before we steamed into Leeds station.

What would have happened if the ticket inspector had not called out each time he was due to appear, I shuddered to think. I wondered what the penalty was for diddling the railway. Mother's eyes were beads of triumph as we dismounted at Leeds but the inspector's popped when he caught sight of me as we walked out of the station.

Dad was there to meet us so I forgot all about Mother's crime in the pleasure of seeing him again. We were hugged and bundled into a taxi. What a journey! Round City Square we went, past the Majestic cinema overlooking the Black Prince and his naked maidens, then along Boar Lane to the Corn Exchange and behind the market which was crowded. I could tell from Mother's silence that she was not impressed by York Road, Compton Road or Harehills Lane, where the streets grew meaner and meaner with row upon row of back-to-back houses blackened with soot and not a blade of grass in sight. We stopped at the first house in Coldcotes Avenue. Despite this name, the district was much inferior to Edgbaston.

'Is this the best you can do?' Mother was on the warpath even before we had walked through the front door. Yet it was a clean, light house with electric lights, not the gas jets we had been used to. Despite that improvement, Mother had made up her mind — the district was awful and it was all Dad's fault. She and Dad had a monumental row before the fire had been lit. However loud her complaints, she was wasting her breath. Dad would not budge an inch. He had rented the house from a customer and the customer was always right.

On Monday we ventured out to explore. As we walked

down the narrow back street running parallel with Harehills Lane, I couldn't help but stare. It was a mild morning so all the doors of the narrow houses were open showing men in their shirt sleeves, braces dangling, pint pots in hand, sitting at tables covered in newspaper tablecloths. Mother had never seen anything like it before and held my hand tightly, as if she expected spears to hurtle in our direction. The only other activity was from a woman scrubbing her front steps then attacking them with a donkey stone.

It was at the Co-op on the shopping parade round the corner that Mother received her second culture shock. 'Some cheese, love? Certainly, love. How much would you like, love? Will that be all, love?' 'Did you ever hear such familiarity, calling me 'love'!' Mother rode her high horse all the way home. She had never before met a Yorkshireman and was ignorant of the dialect and idiom. 'Love' was to Yorkshire shopkeepers as 'Modom' was to Harrods, but it violated her dignity. She found it intolerable.

Higher up Harehills Lane was Brownhill council school. It was huge compared with Mrs Levy's. From Coldcotes Avenue we could hear the children shouting at playtime on weekdays. However frightened I was, I thought the sooner I started there the better, then I should make some friends. I didn't mind being called 'love' as long as I learned to read and whatever else was taught at school.

'When are Bruin and my motor car arriving?' I asked.

'Oh, you're too big for those now – I've sold them.'
It was no good objecting. Mother now wore a perpetual glare, not much of an improvement on her recent crying. All she could say to Dad was, 'I loathe the house. I detest Leeds.' That when she'd only been there a week.

Dad, of course, could escape to work. I had nowhere to go. There were no other children; no garden, muffin

41

man, or rides in the milk cart. Everything was so different. Even the milk came in bottles and Mother had to go far afield to find a kosher butcher. This meant a tram ride as far as the Corn Exchange then a walk up Briggate past Hitchens and Matthias Robinson's until we saw the Dispensary looming. Ragged urchins from Coburg Street and Camp Road ran about barefoot even when snow was on the ground. I enjoyed the smells from Bloomfield's bakery but not the horsey straw-laden air at the Corn Merchant's opposite, where dray horses were taken to feed. You had to be careful where you trod near the horse trough. Mother ignored Mr Harris's butcher's shop as his navy striped apron was always bloodstained. She preferred Mr Rosenhead's shop and so did I as I was sometimes given a raw sausage to eat there. Smuckler's delicatessen nearby was spotless, so we usually called there for salt herrings which were stored in a barrel. Mother, despite her Anglicised upbringing, made delicious chopped herring.

Just behind the Golden Cross public house, there was a Jewish Working Men's Club and the Chevra Thilim Synagogue was not far away in Albert Grove. The Leylands, Carlyle Terrace and the Chapeltown area, including Francis Street, Leopold Street, Lewis Street and up as far as Grange Avenue, were teeming with Jewish immigrants who had fled from the pogroms in Russia. The *goyim* called the North Street park 'Sheeney Park'.

The conversations in Yiddish which she did not understand and the foreign accents did nothing to make Mother feel at home. Although she hated where she had been transplanted, she didn't fancy a ghetto either. For my part I should have preferred it. The liveliness of the foreigners appealed to me and Darley Street and Lovell Road schools would have been an added attraction had I known that the two head masters competed for as many Jewish children as possible. The immigrant families worked hard and were ambitious for their children to have a better life than they had known back in de haim, in Russia. However poor they were, the children were well-fed. It was a common sight for a clutch of Jewish mothers to gather outside these schools at break in order to pass a fish cake or two, still hot from the frying pan, through the railings to their offspring. As the tuition and discipline was first-class and the children were bright, the scholarship success rate at those schools was phenomenal.

I hated leaving North Street behind but on the ride home we passed what I took to be a park. 'Can we go for a walk there at some time?' I asked.

'No, of course not.' Mother sounded quite testy.

I was astonished. 'Why?'

She nudged me hard but I was determined.

'Isn't it a Jewish park?'

At this she went red because she was conditioned only to whisper the word 'Jewish' when amongst Gentiles.

I would not be shushed. I doggedly repeated my question until finally she erupted in a fit of laughter. I was furious. When she got her wind back, she explained, still chuckling to herself as we got off the tram, 'It's a cemetery!'

Eventually Mother found a park practically on our doorstep. There was no lake and the air smelled more of soot than roses but it was better than nothing. I skipped on ahead and passed a park keeper weeding a flower bed. As I went by he looked up, smiled at me, then looked round to see who was with me. Seeing my mother, he rose to his feet and approached her. He touched his forehead before speaking but I couldn't hear what was said. Mother looked upset when she caught up with me.

'A nasty man has been er...frightening little girls so walk near me. And you must never come into the park on

43

your own.' Now there was a hint of danger. What did nasty men do? And why? How I wished I were in school, even the noisy Brownhill nearby would be better than this.

Mother had other ideas for my education. She bought me a copying book and every day sat me with a pencil at the dining-room table. Hour after hour it was 'Thin strokes up and thick ones down' as I copied the alphabet in italics. Row upon row of mind-bending boredom. As this was Mother's only idea of a lesson, I felt I was getting nowhere. I longed to learn how to join the letters into a written word. Most of all, I wanted to be able to read. At five and a half years old I was close to exploding from frustration.

The Indian summer had faded and I had a cold, but nothing worse, when one morning the door bell rang and I saw a gentleman standing there, wearing a bowler hat, navy suit, watch chain across his chest, black boots, and a grave expression. 'I'm from the Board of Education, the Board man,' he announced to Mother, who reluctantly admitted him to the dining-room.

'I understand you have a child here of school age.' he said looking closely at me. My heart leapt. He was important. Mother couldn't very well tell me now to lie down and be covered by a coat. Surely she'd give way? I had a lot to learn about Mother. She was firm as she looked him straight in the eye.

'She's too ill to go out,' she said. 'She has a bad cold, bronchitis, a weak chest..' I expected to hear galloping consumption was next on the list as she glared at me, willing me to cough. I did not oblige. 'And,' Mother was priming her biggest gun, 'I am teaching her myself for the time being.' It was a star performance; she sounded so regal, that the Board man retreated in disarray. I felt desperate.

Dad never seemed to notice that I was old enough for

school, he was so preoccupied with work. He had made many friends during his grass widowhood in Leeds and went out most evenings to play bridge. The wife of one of his friends who lived in Chapeltown invited us for tea one Sunday. It was pleasant enough but the house resembled the one we had left behind in Birmingham so the outing made Mother more homesick than ever. 'I can't bear our house or the district,' she nagged Dad all the way home. He closed his ears. He was adamant we weren't moving.

So Mother retreated into loneliness and clung to me all the more. I had my copying and crayoning books. I also had dolls, of course. They couldn't teach me much. My only hope was the Board man. Fortunately he was persistent and called at weekly intervals. As he was the only person who did call, Mother knew it would be him and ignored the bell. If she stayed out of sight long enough, he gave up. As for me, I was too scared to defy her and tried to keep myself occupied drawing pictures. I found it tantalising that there were dozens of books in the dining-room bureau that I couldn't read. Mother had found a library nearby in Compton Road and passed her evenings knitting and reading. She balanced a book on the arm of her chair, while her fingers manipulated the wool round the needles with piston-like speed. She only stopped to wind another skein of wool which I had to hold on my outstretched arms. Her needles were clicking my time away as I turned over the pages of my comic. How I longed to be able to read it. At this rate I should grow up illiterate with arms permanently stretched from holding wool.

*

Mother was delighted to receive a letter with a Birmingham postmark but put it aside as I had a raging toothache. Dad told Mother of a sixpenny dentist in

Hunslet but, when we got off the tram there, the house looked so seedy only my pain made Mother walk up the path. We were admitted by a man in a greasy frock coat, who turned out to be the dentist. He led us into a back room where the pattern on the wallpaper was obscured by grime. The brown carpet was threadbare and dirty lace curtains filtered whatever light was coming through a narrow window. I was told to sit on a large chair in the middle of the room beside a three foot high, narrow-necked patterned vase acting as a spittoon.

Fear battled with curiosity. How, if ever, was the vase emptied? I had no time to investigate the gruesome depths before I was given a whiff of gas and my tooth was yanked out. The sixpence was paid and we escaped. On our way home, with a scarf round my face to keep out the cold, Mother echoed my thoughts, 'If that's what you get for sixpence,' she said, 'next time, I'll pay a shilling.'

A few days later I held Mother's hand tightly as we walked up Roberts Avenue. It was in the heart of a council estate, not far from our street, but with modern houses and gardens. It was three o'clock in the afternoon. 'A suitable time for calling,' Mother said. She was holding the letter like a talisman. It was from her cousin Lois, giving names and addresses of three Leeds families known to friends in Birmingham. The first name on the list was Jeanne's. Mother's eyes were shining. With an introduction from Birmingham, Jeanne must be alright!

Mother took a deep breath, then rang the doorbell. After a few seconds the door was opened by a young woman. She was tall, with dark wavy hair, fashionably bobbed but not as severe as Mother's Eton Crop, huge brown eyes and a bone structure which would keep her beautiful in old age. She was wearing a short sleeved blue dress with a lace collar, a string of pearls round her neck and a gold slave bangle on her left arm. I had never seen anyone as beautiful since my last visit to Uncle Lewin's cinema. Mother introduced herself and shyly waved the letter. Jeanne invited us inside. Oh how I prayed she wouldn't call Mother 'love'. Peering round her skirt was a little girl, a pixie with small features and her mother's dark eyes and hair. Within five minutes we were all comfortable in the living room. The little girl, Vivienne, showed me her tea-set, and we played round a dining chair, using it as a table while our mothers chattered ten to the dozen. Jeanne made Mother laugh when she described how, after she had recently dared to have her long hair bobbed, she wore a mob cap for a week to hide it from her husband.

He was the chief violinist at the Rialto cinema in town. His artistic temperament might have been responsible for one eccentricity: Vivienne was not allowed access to any mirror, even in her small hand bag, in case she became conceited. I sighed. She was very pretty. No-one seemed to think they should apply the same restriction to me. She had many talents and one was for getting attention. When she became bored with our game, she lay down on the floor, straight and stiff, closed her eyes and announced loudly, 'I'm dead!' That stopped the conversation and threw both mothers into a tizzy. I was impressed but didn't think I could get away with that. After all, I was five and a half and expected to know better.

Before we left, a future meeting was arranged. It was the first time for months that I had seen Mother happy. She had found a friend. As I skipped beside her on the way home, she was humming *Ain't she sweet*. So as we passed Brownhill school, sensing her change of mood, I tentatively mentioned for the hundredth time the question of school. 'When you're better,' Mother replied. Better! I fumed but kept quiet. Grown-ups were unpredictable.

Dad would be home from work soon and that would make a diversion, providing his supper was edible. Mother bothered very little about looking after him and nowadays froze when she heard his footsteps. To make matters worse, he was banished to the back bedroom and Mother had moved me in with her. It was sad but Dad never told me stories any more. Rather he stormed in and blazed out again after being served a congealed dinner with a request for money. Mother picked her moments. Why were my parents different from every one else's? There were times when I despaired.

I put it all behind me a few days later when we called on Mrs Rose, the second name in Mother's letter. She lived in Sholebroke Avenue where the air smelled sweeter than in our neighbourhood. I knew as soon as we approached the house with trees and shrubs in the garden that Mother would be nostalgic for Birmingham. Mrs Rose had been a teacher before she had married. She was an imposing, no-nonsense woman, with gold-rimmed spectacles and her hair done up in a bun.

There was no-one for me to play with so I was soon bored stiff. It was difficult sitting still without fidgetting when the conversation was stilted, with no gossip or juicy snippets. Even Mother looked relieved when Mrs Rose disappeared to make the tea. These refreshments were a treat; home-made cake, scones and jam, and scrumptious crescent biscuits. I enjoyed my fourth but the look in Mother's eye ruled out a fifth. After tea I sat back expecting to spend the rest of the visit counting the ridges on the heavily carved sideboard, when Mrs Rose murmured about 'finding something for idle hands.' After foraging in a work box, she produced a pair of knitting needles and some wool. 'Now, let's see if you can knit.' Mother was beaming. She had never thought of teaching me her favourite hobby.

Mrs Rose was a born teacher and bossed my podgy

fingers into holding the needles, torturing the wool round the pointed end, making a loop and sliding the stitch off. Then again and again and again. I felt no affinity with knitting like Mother had but I did feel a sense of achievement at having learnt something. I did so well that I wondered if there were any chance of Mrs Rose teaching me to read but although we had been made most welcome, I could tell that Mother and Mrs Rose had little in common except knitting. The relationship would not be pursued.

The following week, still clutching the same letter, we walked down Harehills Lane and turned right into the maze of through terraced houses. It was a crisp autumn day with a hint of fog and soot in the air. We stopped at what we hoped was the right door. The pocket handkerchief sized garden was tended and the lace curtains and aspidistra in the window looked promising.

The door was opened by Mary, a small dark woman in her late thirties. Her sallow features lit up with a warm smile showing beautiful teeth when she heard Mother's introduction of who was related to whom and without any further to-do we were invited in. She limped and I longed to ask her why but knew I'd catch it if I did. Mary had one son, who was elsewhere when we arrived. She paused at the bottom of the steep, unlit staircase to call up, 'Henry! Have you been?' There was a muffled answer.

'Right, you can come down, now.'

Henry was almost my age and also not at school. He, too, sneezed occasionally and was another delicate child. It was obvious the two ladies had plenty in common, even more so as Alf, Mary's husband, had a job with a film company, which not only sounded glamorous but promised plenty of free trade-show tickets.

The ladies were settled in the kitchen, waiting for the kettle to boil on the open range. Henry and I were sent to play in the front room, which was dark, smelt of furniture polish and had a green plush tablecloth on the large table. A small stand in the window was the home of the aspidistra which blocked out most of the light. I stood looking round at the brown patterned carpet, parquet patterned lino surround and dark brown paint. There was a fan of paper in the grate but not a toy in sight. Henry was sturdily built, with mournful brown eyes which could light up from mischief, straight brown hair cut in a fringe and a grin which stretched from ear to ear. I looked at him and wondered what on earth we were going to play. We tried a mild form of cowboys and Indians round the table, with me keeping a sharp eye on the aspidistra, but finally flopped on to the scratchy horsehair-covered dining chairs and swung our legs in silence.

After a few moments Henry jumped up and said, 'Just watch this,' and before I could gasp 'Crikey!' he was standing in front of the hearth, expertly aiming above the pleated white paper and peeing away into the grate. The feat was even more impressive because he could do it without looking, his head swivelled round, roaring with laughter at my shocked expression.

A minute later, his mother looked round the door to ask, 'Are you sure you've been, Henry?' He looked angelic as he assured her he had indeed been.

'Let me know whatever you hear about that school,' Mother said in farewell. So they'd been discussing education, our education? From what I could gather, it appeared there was a private school on Roundhay Road eminently more suitable for delicate only children than the hurly-burly of the council school on our doorstep. In the next few days Mother was going to inspect it, then she and Mary would confer on the matter. She also liked the sound of the uniform.

What a bonanza of a day! I had met a daring, naughty

boy, who looked as if butter wouldn't melt in his mouth, and there was progress on the educational front! Mother was at least talking of sending me to school.

*

I could hardly believe that I was really standing in Miss Starfield's outfitting shop at Sheepscar trying on a gymslip. It felt scratchy and smelt of new wool, as did the blazer. They were both a mellow brown with a gold embroidered badge on the blazer pocket. As thrilled as Cinders, I stroked the matching tie. 'Do stand still!' Mother pleaded, while the gymslip hem was being measured. Miss Starfield, a small, quiet lady, was on her knees with her mouth full of pins. I hoped she wouldn't swallow any. I tried on a brown gaberdine raincoat followed by a velour hat which also sported a badge.

'I'd put an elastic on the hat, if I were you,' Miss Starfield suggested to Mother. My heart sank. One twang of a hat elastic and my neck would hurt for a week.

'We won't be needing any socks,' Mother said. Oh no! that meant the needles would be clicking non-stop but I'd endure anything if I were starting school.

'And you'll have to have an elastic sewn on your hat, whether you like it or not,' Mother said on our way home. By the time we've bought you some shoes, there'll be no change out of five pounds, so I don't want you losing your hat in the first puff of wind.' I didn't say a word. A fiver! That was half Dad's wage for a week!

When Dad arrived home that evening, Mother opened fire with, 'You owe me five pounds for Joan's uniform.'

He looked at his dinner: re-heated dark brown stew congealing on an enamel plate.

Mother nagged on. 'And before she starts school, you'll have to take her for a haircut. I'm not trailing round this Godforsaken slum looking for a hairdresser. You're making me live here. You can do it.' She paused for breath and took the clothing bill from her handbag. Dad, with a roar of rage, picked up the plate of food and threw it at her. Fortunately his aim was bad and it landed on the lino. I escaped to my bedroom in order to miss the rest of the slanging match and only ventured down when Dad had gone out. Mother was on her knees, clearing up the mess. She had been crying. 'Your father's in one of his usual tempers,' she said, her expression one of injured innocence.

*

On Sunday Dad took me to get my hair cut. Mother still had her Eton Crop cut at a town salon but why she had not taken me with her, I never found out.

I felt out of place in the barber's shop amongst the men hidden under steaming white towels. 'Having their beauty treatment,' Dad laughed. I was surprised they could breathe. Another was having a cut-throat shave but without any accompanying aria. Bay rum and tobacco spiced the hubbub of racing talk. The customers waiting their turn swapped jokes amidst guffaws of laughter until Dad said, 'Turn it up. There's a child in here.' Then, as they were all Jewish, he told some jokes in Yiddish which he knew I didn't understand. The barber laughed so much he had to stop shaving. Dad certainly hadn't lost his flair for entertaining.

'You must have a lot of fun at home,' the barber said to me when he had dried his eyes. I smiled and kept quiet. They should only know.

Then it was my turn. The barber was young, handsome and looked so nice that I trusted him. Snip, snip, snip and five minutes later, I had a boy's short back-and-sides. I had not cried once when the dreaded clippers' cold steel touched me, although this time I had something to cry about. They had ploughed round my neck, in front of my ears and onto my cheeks. Now superfluous hair would grow on my face.

I was furious with Mother but when we got home she never even noticed I had a boy's haircut. She must have thought that Eton Crops were also the latest for little girls. I had one consolation. There were three weeks to go before school started. If I pulled my hair every day, by then I might look almost female.

Chapter Three

Monday brought excitement which took my mind off my hair. At the time when Dad was due home there was a backfiring noise outside the house. I looked out and there he was, grinning proudly, at the wheel of a large Citroen. It was as square as a tank, with steel rails along the inside of the roof, but the loveliest sight in Harehills. I raced down the front steps and he let me in beside him. He drove up and down the street bucking like a bronco, crashing the gears and swearing until eventually he got the hang of it. 'I'll have to watch out for the robots,' he said, meaning traffic lights. Leeds was the first place to have them. Nobody else nearby had a car so there was no problem with parking. When Mother came out to see what all the fuss was about, even she was impressed although she carped, 'But can you afford it?'

'It's Hobson's choice.' He explained that his cousin was branching out from furs into the *'shmatte'* business, cheap dresses and coats. In future Dad was going to travel round Yorkshire to the towns and villages big enough to boast a gown shop. Most drapers also sold dresses. It would mean harder work for him, heaving all the samples in and out of the car and more time away from home.

'What a cheapskate your cousin is, expecting you to buy your own car,' Mother said. I held my breath, ready to run upstairs. Yet although she could not resist a dig, Mother treated the news of Dad's travelling with ill-concealed delight. With him away, we should have a quiet house from Monday to Friday, free from screaming and shouting. Dad, she told me, was going to start in two week's time after Christmas.

In the meantime at Chanuchah, the Festival of Lights,

Mother lit the candles in the Menorah. In our home, this festival was not celebrated by an exchange of gifts as in an orthodox house. Instead I was allowed to hang up my socks on Christmas Eve which would have given Grandpa a stroke if he'd known. Mother and Father, however, gave presents at Rosh Hashanah, our New Year, when Dad usually bought me gloves and gave Mother 4711 Cologne, and Mother knitted Dad a scarf or something similarly useful. At that time, I received no pocket money so I had not learnt the pleasure of giving presents.

This Chanuchah, as far as I was concerned, was different and I was in for a surprise. 'I've something for you,' Mother said and handed me a parcel. I hoped it wasn't some relic from her own childhood, like her favourite doll made of leather, carefully wrapped and given me one Christmas morning. I had thought it old fashioned and worse, had never loved it. And that had made me feel guilty. But this present wasn't anything like that. It was a book, beautifully illustrated in colour, of Bible stories specially simplified for children. I was delighted and longed to be able to read it.

*

I was up early, dressed in my new uniform, and apprehensive. For a six-and-a-half year old it was a long hike in the cold down Bayswater Road to Priory School. The narrow streets were strung with washing, a bunting of long johns, nighties, bloomers and sheets ballooning in the wind and gathering smuts from the belching chimneys, but at last we reached Roundhay Road. There we crossed over to a small yard where a flight of iron steps led up to the school.

Miss Elsie, the principal, thin nosed and her hair in earphones, received us. There were a lot of children, all shapes and sizes, surging past, far more than I had been used to at Mrs Levy's. I was scared stiff. Mother told Miss Elsie I was to have school dinners but not pork, ham or shellfish. I felt embarrassed at being different.

'Oh, and one other thing,' Mother was also looking uncomfortable, 'are your prayers suitable for a Jewish child?'

Miss Elsie looked over the top of her gold-rimmed glasses and pursed her lips. 'Our prayers are suitable for any child,' she said. There was a chill in the air. Mother kissed me goodbye and abandoned me in the corridor which also doubled as a cloakroom.

The room next door was packed with about sixty boys and girls sitting in rows shuffling their feet and chattering. A hush fell as Miss Elsie took the register. I was seated on the front row with the smaller children.

'Who wants milk?' Miss Elsie asked. I squirmed and put my hand up.

'I don't like milk!' I blurted.

'You are only to say if you wish to buy milk at break,' Miss Elsie answered with an expression which said, 'Dim-wit!' I shrank back and hoped to die. There seemed to be a million things I didn't know as well as my three 'Rs'.

A short prayer was said mentioning Jesus once or twice which made me feel uneasy. When it came to singing my mind was distracted by a rollicking good tune. I threw myself into it with gusto for the words were so easy to remember. It was some sort of army song.

A bell was rung and Miss Hilda shepherded me into another large room, towards the end which was the 'babies' class. I leaned forward waiting eagerly. What was I going to learn? Exercise books were handed out and pencils. But when I opened my book it was only to find pages and pages of letters all sloping in uniform rows, waiting to be copied. Thin up, thick down, thin up, thick down. I had been doing that for months. At the other end of the room, a class of older children were chanting their tables. Twice-two-are-four, multiplied by twenty voices, lifted the ceiling. Although I tried to block out the noise, it was impossible to concentrate. When Miss Hilda saw my work she smiled and told me I'd done quite well for my first go. I had the sense, for once, not to tell her I'd already filled three similar books for Mother.

Then it was lunch time. Now what was I supposed to do? Mother had emphasised my home would be judged by my table manners. 'Whatever you do, don't talk with your mouth full' was still ringing in my ears.

A trestle table in the third classroom had been laid with a white cloth, cutlery and glasses. Twenty children and staff, headed by Miss Elsie, sat down. She looked round the table, her face moist and shiny as she pushed her glasses further up her nose. 'Can anyone here say grace?'

'I can, Miss Elsie,' I said.

'Then proceed,' she said, sitting back with her hands folded in her lap and her eyes cast down.

I felt very important and intoned, loud and clear, 'For what I have received, may the Lord make me truly grateful. Now please may I leave the table?'

There was a roar of laughter. Too late, it dawned. There was such a thing as grace-before-meals and 'Please-can-I-leave-the-table?' was not a religious codicil. I blushed, mortified down to my socks, but still managed to enjoy the roast beef and two veg, followed by sponge pudding and custard. It was better than Mondays at home.

In the afternoon, when Miss Elsie was giving us a drawing lesson, there was a knock on the door, and I was astonished to see our Board man walk in. Miss Elsie gave him the register to inspect, and after making a note of any absentees, he murmured some pleasantry about the weather then departed. This exchange had surprised me. When Miss Elsie came to look at my drawing, I said, 'When that man calls at our house, my Mother doesn't answer the door.'

'Then your mother is a very rude woman!' said Miss Elsie with a sniff. I'd done it this time. Mother would be furious when she heard.

But Mother did not hear how I had let her down for when she collected me, she was too aghast by my rendition of the marching song to enquire about anything else. I sang at the top of my voice as I skipped along beside her, 'Onward Christian soldiers, marching as to war!'

Mother may have been at odds with her father but she drew the line at me singing hymns. After that I had to sit in the corridor during prayers, gazing at the tiles on the wall, listening to the lusty singing, and feeling isolated. If I was different, so be it.

Every day Mother and I had the long trek backwards and forwards to school with no trees or gardens to divert us. It was fortunate we were used to walking because the General Strike crippled all public transport for ten days soon after I had started there. When Mother wanted to shop in the market we had to walk there. If a tram came by at all, the fares were collected by a 'civilian' in a lounge suit.

Meanwhile, I managed to keep out of further trouble at school, having learnt a little of tact and diplomacy. Unfortunately, I had not learned much else. History was mostly taught as a list of dates and geography was non-existent. As I had a talent for drawing, I was given some laburnum to copy, day in and day out. The sketches must have impressed Miss Elsie, as she entered one for an examination and I was awarded a certificate of merit. Mother was very proud. My first term's report was glowing so Mother never heard of the two-classes-per-room and the difficulty I had in concentrating, nor did she realise I could barely write my name.

Yet despite the noise in the classroom, something must have sunk in. One Sunday, I was sitting on a stool at Mother's knee, looking at the pictures in my comic which she was reading to me. Dad was in an armchair, immersed in the paper.

'Sinbad the sailor went to sea...' Mother was an excellent, expressive reader. I could smell the ozone, feel the boat rock. My eyes strayed down to the text and my stomach lurched from excitement. Instead of seeing meaningless hieroglyphics, the letters had suddenly sorted themselves into words. Words which I understood. I interrupted Mother.

'Wait!' I said, then continued, 'Sinbad raised the sails, and steered the ship away from the storm.'

I hugged Mother with delight. It was as if a piece of a jigsaw had been slotted into place inside my head. The feeling was exhilarating.

The next day, Mother took me to the library at Compton Road and I was given my first library tickets. They opened a new world for me.

*

By the time I was ten, I had read most of the books in Mother's bureaux except the *Rubaiyat of Omar Khayyam*, which she said was most unsuitable. Mrs Molesworthy's *Carrots, Just A Little Boy* was my favourite so I read it over and over again. The book of Bible stories I saved for the Holy days. I could easily understand the text and the coloured illustrations by Arthur A. Dixon leapt from the page. They interpreted the stories so well. Nothing like the fiction in Mother's *Home Notes*, the Bible stories were wonderful and terrible; tales of passion, hatred, deprivation and hardship which fired my imagination as nothing else had done. I shuddered at Jacob and Esau's jealousy and agonised each time I read that Moses was hidden in the bulrushes in case the basket floated away and he was discovered by Pharaoh. I relished Samson's strength, Daniel's courage and Solomon's wisdom and marvelled at the love of family and forgiveness which distinguished Joseph. The biggest surprise for me was that Joseph was shown dressed in flowing robes. I had visualised him as a little boy in a tailored coat made up of patchwork.

That I was a bookworm and also getting good reports from school, must have prompted Mother to think of sending me to a high school. Eventually she made an appointment to see Miss Scotson Clark, the headmistress of Chapel Allerton High School but it came to nothing as Mother was horrified by the fees.

'We can't possibly afford to send you there,' she told me. 'It costs eighteen guineas a year and extra for books and games.' That was a disappointment as I wanted more than anything to go to a high school.

Mother said nothing to me but tackled Dad at the weekend with an eye to improving our finances. 'You're flogging yourself to death, working for Nat. Why not go into business for yourself? You know where to go for stock — Nat often sends you buying. You have a car. Why not give it a go?'

I stole a glance at Dad. His jaw had dropped.

'But I don't want to get into a mess like last time.' He was thinking of the Birmingham shop and the bad debts it had taken two years to pay off.

'You won't. You know this business inside out. And you've the gift of the gab. You won't fail this time.'

Dad gave Mother a sharp look at the 'gift of the gab' comment, but when he saw she was not being sarcastic, he continued, 'What shall I do for capital? We'll have to live on something. The bank won't lend without security.'

'You can borrow on the money Uncle Manny left me until you get going.' This was a big concession as Mother regarded her small inheritance as very much her own.

Dad found a piece of paper and spent the next half hour totting up figures. 'I'm scared stiff of the responsibility,' he said finally. 'I'll have to borrow at least three hundred pounds.'

'Take the plunge,' Mother said. She must have been thinking of her father and all her enterprising uncles. Their motto was 'The best person to work for is yourself.'

There were further discussions over the weekend. Then Dad decided that Mother was right and he gave in his notice. He found a room in Briggate House over Horne Brothers, hired a young lady to be his secretary, then bought some rails and enough stock to fill them. The office was the cheapest room in the building, on the top floor next to the lavatory. During the first week while Dad was travelling, the secretary nearly went mad from boredom. No-one crossed the threshold and all she could hear all day was the sound of the toilet flushing! In that time she knitted two sleeves and the back of a jumper and was about to give notice when the first customer called. Then the orders started coming in and the business was launched. Dad never regretted following Mother's advice and his secretary stayed for over twenty years.

In the early days of the business, high school fees were still out of the question, but one day fate intervened in the shape of the Board man. I was off school with a cold when he called. I had long since confessed to Mother that I had shopped her to Miss Elsie, so now Mother always admitted him and on this day, in a rare burst of familiarity, she offered him a cup of tea. As they sat together she also confided her worries about my further education. Despite his black boots and bowler hat, he was a guardian angel. He not only overlooked Mother's previous rudeness but after patiently listening, proved to be a fount of information and common sense. If his help were coals of fire, Mother never acknowledged it. There was a Junior City Scholarship, he told us, open to pupils from council schools. 'Why not', he suggested, 'apply for your daughter to sit, even if she is at a private school? After all, you pay your rates like everybody else!'

Mother immediately did as he had advised, and in due course, permission was granted.

'Joan's a bright girl,' Miss Elsie assured my delighted mother. 'She'll walk it, I'm sure.'

I was to be the first girl in Leeds from a private school to sit for this examination, although I had never before sat for anything harder than the drawing exam, and that was when I was six. But what had I to worry about? They all thought I was clever so I was beginning to believe it myself. How I wanted that scholarship!

The week of the examination came round and so did a 'flu epidemic. For three days before the exam, I sweated and coughed in bed. For once I was really ill and Mother was frantic. All she could do, apart from dosing me with the doctor's potion and rubbing my chest with camphorated oil, was read to me. She picked *Uncle Tom's Cabin*. That made me feel even worse. On the day of the exam I kept quiet that I still felt ill, and dressed ready to set out. Dad drove me to Thoresby High School.

The classroom was upstairs. I started to climb in my usual fashion: two at a time, but before I reached the top I had to hold on to the banister as the stairs spun round and round. Before the papers were doled out I felt like a jelly but after I had looked at the sums, I dissolved altogether. The problems were way over my head, far harder than anything I had been taught at Priory. I had a good stab at the composition with 'A day in the country', but I could not answer many of the history questions. I knew a jumble of dates and little else, other than that King Alfred had burnt some cakes, and Canute had tried something daft with the tide. Those double classes had a lot to answer for. The sweat ran down my palms and I was red from anxiety, not triumph, when Mother collected me.

I crawled into bed with a hot drink as soon as I reached home. Not even Mother reading *What Katie Did At School* could console me for my miserable performance. I knew in my aching bones I should not be going to a high school.

∗

I was right all too soon. The Board man was sitting on the edge of one of our dining chairs, silently sympathising that I had not been awarded a scholarship. Next year I should be three months too old to try again. He gazed into his cup of tea as if seeking inspiration. 'You know', he looked up at Mother, 'as Joan had the 'flu during the exam, you could get a doctor's certificate to say so, then they might let her sit again next year. It's worth a try.' Mother perked up at this. He continued, 'But I do recommend that if they allow her to have another go, you send her to Brownhill. It's a very good school with one of the best scholarship classes in Leeds. The form mistress is a bit of a Tartar but she gets results.'

Ever practical, Mother lost no time in calling on the doctor and returned clutching the vital certificate stating that I had been unfit at the time of the examination. She then sat down and composed a letter on her best notepaper to the Department of Education. Would they grant the dispensation? All we could do was hope.

∗

Mother began to look on Coldcotes Avenue as a jinx and nagged even harder to move. 'Nothing doing,' Dad snapped. 'Not while the landlord owns three gown shops.'

Every time Mother passed the large damp patch on the landing ceiling, she averted her eyes as if from some obscenity, muttering, 'Revolting! No wonder I feel ill.' I knew this meant there would be another row later. The quarrels were sickening. If only there could be a truce.

Mother and I were in considerable pain. All my joints hurt and on some days I could hardly raise my arms. 'Just growing pains,' the doctor dismissed with a shrug. He could hardly say the same to Mother and prescribed Fynnon salts for her. Mother dosed me with Angiers' Emulsion which tasted of furniture polish. To make matters worse, I had a cough and was made to swallow Malto Yerbine, a vile brew, four times a day, and wear a piece of flannel on my chest.

Matters came to a head one Sunday. It started like any other Sunday. Dad was still in bed, snoring like an ungreased engine missing on two cylinders. Every few minutes, in between massive snorts, he stopped breathing, then, just when I thought he'd died, a strangled gasp escaped. I was dressed and in the dining-room, reading my comic. It was peaceful downstairs with only the comforting sound of Mother humming a snatch of *Velia* as she pottered in the kitchen. If I looked up, I could see her through the doorway, her short hair brushed straight back from her flushed face and her ample frame in a maroon jumper and skirt under a striped pinafore made from one of Dad's old shirts. There was a delicious smell of roast meat and cloves, which meant baked apples, our usual Sunday pudding. I didn't mind the apples but hated the cloves. The table was laid with an embroidered white cloth.

'You'd better go and wake your father, the dinner's

nearly ready,' Mother called round the door in a tone which implied, 'Some people can sleep all day, while I have to work!' That was unfair. Whatever Dad's faults, he was not lazy and in my opinion, entitled to a lie-in once a week. I hesitated, anxious to finish what I was reading.

Suddenly, there was a commotion from the direction of the chimney. I looked up, just as a blackbird crashed down and launched a ton of soot into the room. I let out a scream; a bird swooping down on me was one of my nightmares. That brought Mother rushing in from the kitchen and she threw up her hands in horror. The bird was flapping all round the room, trying to get out, in the meantime creating a pall of soot. Mother did the obvious and rushed to open the sash window, but as it had not been opened for years, it wouldn't budge.

The more the bird flew at me, the louder I screamed, rooted to the spot. When I managed to unlock my legs, I escaped into the hall where I found Dad, his hair on end as he staggered down the stairs, stuffing his pyjama top into his trousers while trying to avoid tripping over his braces. 'What on earth's going on?' he gasped. 'From the racket you're making, I thought the house was on fire!'

By now he was at the dining-room door. He opened it and gasped again. The bird was still hurtling round against the walls, whirling soot like an electric fan. Mother was still pitting her strength against the window. Dad for once was needed. He rushed over, bent down and gave a mighty heave. The frame gave a fraction, then another until there was a gap large enough to admit some cleaner air and provide an escape route. The bird needed no tempting to leave; it was as glad to see the back of us, as we were of it.

When it had left I calmed down but fully expected Dad to explode. It was then, and not for the first time, that I discovered how unpredictable my parents could be. Mother shook the tablecloth out of the window, then turned it over, wiped the cutlery, and in silence, re-laid the table. Dad was wielding a dustpan and broom. I was coughing from the soot so for the moment did not hear the noise. Mother and Dad looked at each other, then ran into the kitchen. Water was pouring through the ceiling. The floor was awash. To avoid the water I went into the hall. 'Dad! Dad!' I yelled. At this he came running to see what I was making another fuss about. A waterfall was cascading down the stairs. The tank had burst and no-one knew where the stop-tap was.

Mother sat down on a dining chair, her lips set in a mutinous line. She wiped her hands on her apron. 'You can rescue the dinner,' she said to Dad, 'I've had enough.'

Without a word, he paddled into the hall, took his umbrella out of the hallstand, opened it and went into the kitchen which resembled Roundhay Park lake. With umbrella in one hand and the roasting dish of meat and potatoes in the other, he served the lunch. He had to make three journeys for the cabbage, carving knife and fork, serving spoon and plates, before he could sit down.

The meal was eaten in silence with Mother and Dad staring woodenly ahead. I was dying to laugh but stifled it. Neither seemed to think serving up the dinner from under an umbrella was unusual. But if Dad were not laughing he was at least doing a bit of hard thinking. After he had rescued the baked apples, he sat down at the desk, pulled down the flap and took the top off his fountain pen. 'How much time will you need to find another house?' he said to Mother over his shoulder. He was quite dignified in defeat. 'How much notice shall I give?'

At the word 'Notice' Mother gave a gasp of joy.

'A month!' Her voice was radiant. 'Just give me a month!' Then Mother did something unprecedented in our four years in Leeds. She picked her way over the debris and gave Dad a voluntary, sooty kiss.

*

Mother's legs were buckling. Dad had sent us to look at a bungalow going for six hundred pounds on Alwoodley Lane. It had been built by a friend of his so Mother had her doubts before we set off. She had had more than enough of Dad's obsessive fear of offending a customer and he might be even worse dealing with a friend. Mother was also uneasy about the cost of mortgage repayments and repairs when Dad's business was only just paying its way.

The walk from Moortown up Harrogate Road had taken nearly an hour. Then there was a trek along Alwoodley Lane, which was little more than a country road with an infrequent bus service. Fortunately, the sun was shining as we trudged past cows grazing in the fields. We paused to admire several mansions overlooking Eccup reservoir before we finally reached the bungalow. It was at the top of a steep drive, and had an unusual glass dome set in the middle of the roof. It looked delightful and the setting was idyllic. Mother leaned against the garden wall. Beads of perspiration glistened on her top lip.

'I wouldn't mind going in just to have a sit-down,' she said, 'but it's no good. I couldn't live as far out as this. Can you imagine walking this distance, carrying shopping, when there's snow on the ground?' I groaned in sympathy. My legs also felt like rubber. So we turned round and hiked back to Moortown Corner. Mother looked relieved when a tram clanged into view. 'I'm going to tell your Dad I can't tackle a marathon like this every day!' She had missed buying a bargain in what became, within a few years, a prestigious suburb with buses, shops, and all mod cons, but she never seemed to regret it.

That was the first of many such excursions and Mother had still not found anywhere for us to live when Auntie Mary told her that there were some houses to rent in Copgrove Road, not far from Harehills Parade. Mother went to inspect and met me at tea-time delighted with what she had found. The houses were brand new with gardens and there was one left at a pound a week rent. When Dad came home at the weekend, he signed the lease without a murmur.

On Saturday Mother celebrated by taking me to a matinee at the Rialto cinema. Everyone was talking about Al Jolson in *The Singing Fool*. The house was packed to hear Jolson sing. I had seen *The Jazz Singer*, but that had been mostly silent. No-one had been sure whether talkies would catch on. I sat there entranced as Jolson pulled out all the stops. As usual when I was watching a film, I believed it was all real. I was fine until his baby boy died. Then Jolson sang *Climb Upon My Knee, Sonny Boy*, and the sight of the angelic child floating in a Hollywood heaven set me off. I was heartbroken and started to sob. I cried for Jolson, his little boy and Mother's lost baby, throughout the rest of the film. I was still weeping while we were waiting for a tram and cried all the way home. Faced with my tears, all Mother could repeat at frequent intervals was, 'Don't be upset, it's only a film!'

I was agog on removal day as we drove up Copgrove Road. The houses were all modern, with, as Mother kept repeating to us, 'Casement windows.' I had no idea what this meant but was soon enlightened. There would be no more struggling with heavy sash windows or broken cords. Our house was nearly at the top of the hill, which was so steep that the houses opposite towered over the main road. Their gardens were sloping terraces.

I was the first out of the car, nearly falling over my feet

as I rushed up the steep drive to explore. Our lawn also sloped but upwards. The incline wouldn't spoil it for playing on and Mother had promised me a swing.

Once inside I was warned not to get in the way of the removal men who were due any second so I went into the kitchen to help Mother wash out the dresser next to the chimney-breast. Dad was trying to light a fire and it was obvious he had never been a Boy Scout. 'Oh, leave it to me, you're hopeless!' Mother snapped, and I held my breath. Fortunately, the fire caught and saved the situation.

Soon, the furniture was carried in and Mother followed the men around, supervising. Up in her bedroom, she was not too pleased to find a chip out of her marble-topped wash stand but the flowered chamberpot had survived. My white bedroom suite went into the back bedroom which overlooked the garden. I ran down to watch the brown plush velvet sofa and armchairs being trundled into a front room which was light and quite spacious. The dining-room furniture just fitted into the back room, where most of the light was blocked by the steep garden. Back in the kitchen I helped Mother unload the saucepans and crockery. There was plenty of room for our big table and chairs, Mother's armchair and her huge wooden-rollered mangle.

Mother hummed *Tea for two* as she made tea for everyone. I couldn't abide the stuff, after Dad had once made me an over-sugared cup so I drank water. Mother gave the large white sink an extra rub, and stood back and admired the electric cooker which was already installed. I thought she might dance, as well as sing, she was so pleased with everything. Later in my room, which looked out on to trees and the garden, I just had time before I fell asleep to wonder what the neighbours would be like and if there were any children nearby.

We now lived much nearer to Priory school and – top

luxury! — there was a tram stop down a steep flight of steps, only a hundred yards away. Unfortunately, this was one stop past the fare stage, which was at the bottom of the hill where there was a parade of shops and the newly-built Clock Cinema.

The next morning Dad drove me to school. At four o'clock I felt very grown-up as I had been given permission to bring myself home from now on. I walked part of the way with Elsie, whose aunt had just had a baby. I knew by now that babies were not brought in the doctor's black bag. But how one got into the stomach in the first place and then out again, was a real mystery.

'Oh, I know the answer to that one,' said Elsie, with a confident air. I stopped walking and looked at her, hanging on every word.

'They cut open your stomach, and get it out through the belly button, of course.' I shook my head in amazement. It sounded horrific but that did not stop me dreaming, all the way home of how much better it would be to have a real baby to cuddle instead of a doll.

As I ran up Copgrove Road enjoying the trees and gardens, I marvelled that the air smelled so fresh. I was even happier at the sight of a tall woman with three handsome sons, one of whom was my age, going up the path of the semi attached to ours. I was just about to smile when the woman glared at me and rushed them all inside. As I walked up our path, I glanced at their window. The handsome quartet were all grimacing, thumbs to their noses, waggling their fingers at me. I felt sick and went inside. Father's reaction was, 'Bloody anti-semites!' They continued to show their hostility in this way whenever they saw us. We ignored it. Neither family ever exchanged a word.

In the meantime Mother got out her sewing machine and beavered away making curtains. There was blue and white folk-weave at two-and-eleven a yard for the dining-room and my bedroom, and a leaf-patterned brown rayon for the lounge. We already had carpet squares with parquet patterned lino surrounds. Mother had chosen a mauve square for her bedroom and had managed to find some matching lino. It looked well with the mahogany furniture.

In a couple of weeks we were straight. During all this upheaval, the question of my education had taken a back seat. Now I started to worry again — what would the outcome be?

*

Mother's fingers were all thumbs as she wrestled with an envelope, which had Department of Education printed on it. Then her face broke into a smile and she hugged me. I was to be allowed to sit next year despite being over-age. I was delighted then plunged into terror. I could only read, write and draw. History and geography were closed books and, as for arithmetic, I hardly knew my tables. I should be roasted alive at Brownhill under the 'bit of a Tartar.' There was no alternative if I were to have a chance.

Before I left Priory, Mother made me a belated birthday party and eight of my school friends came to tea. Unfortunately I was in an evil mood as Mother had embarrassed me by booking Arthur Leo, a professional entertainer, to give a Punch and Judy show. I was eleven, for goodness sake, not six! Still, everyone else seemed to enjoy themselves, so I eventually brightened up and Mother never noticed I had been sulking.

After the guests had gone, I opened my presents on the kitchen table. Besides a birthday book, an autograph book and a manicure set, there was, to my delight, *Alice Through The Looking-Glass* and *Little Women*. Stella and

72

Lolita, who were Turkish, had brought a well-wrapped two-pound box of scrumptious French chocolates but when it was opened there were four chocolates missing from the middle! Their Mama must have tucked in before parting with them. Our laughter dispelled my black cloud completely. We agreed the party had been a great success but it never occurred to me to thank Mother for making it.

Three weeks later we broke up. No more classes two-to-a-room, no more drawing laburnum. I could go out to play and get to know the neighbours. The family in the house which adjoined our drive was, thank heaven, friendly. The son, Roger, tinkered with his motor-bike all his spare time, taking it to pieces, then putting it back together again. His mother, Mrs Reid, although a kindly, pleasant person, was roughly spoken with untidy hair and a florid complexion. Mr Reid, on the other hand, was tall, good looking, with sleek hair and a cultured accent. He was a commercial traveller and, like Dad, was away a lot. I heard Mother telling Auntie Jeanne Mr Reid had lodged with Mrs Reid's parents. Then her voice dropped to a muffled whisper, 'and they had to get married.' However oddly matched the Reids were, at least they chatted to us about the weather when we met.

Poor Mrs Reid! One afternoon when no-one was in, I answered the back door to find a constable on the step, asking for her. He told me Mr Reid had had a heart attack and had died on board the London-Midland-Scottish train. I heard when I was much older that Mrs Reid had received another shock. Her husband had kept an 'office' in town, furnished with a sofa and a supply of contraceptives.

Dorothy lived on the other side of the road. She was my age and we played happily together, pushing our dolls' prams up the street. Her pram was far nicer than mine. How I envied her! We only had one argument which was never resolved. She could not accept that I was English. 'You can't be if you're Jewish!' she insisted. I felt uncomfortable, was I so different?

Irene, who was staying with her Aunt two doors away, was also happy to play with me. It was the first time since we had lived in Leeds that I could go out to play with other children. I was welcome in their homes and they in mine.

Mother's social life was also picking up. She was invited to a tea-party two doors away. The table was laid beautifully, groaning with several large, uncut cakes. The sandwiches were passed round, then the hostess announced, 'Do help yourselves to cake; any that are left over are for sale!' The guests, including Mother, were so flabbergasted, they hadn't the courage to cut any of the cakes, in case they were ruining their hostess's profit. They didn't buy any, either.

Mother had other things on her mind. Her teeth were giving her a lot of trouble and she was told she would have to have them out. The following Friday morning, Mother sat in an armchair in our front room, while the doctor administered the anaesthetic and the dentist pulled out her teeth. When they left, Mother felt and looked so groggy, spitting blood into a bowl, that I was scared stiff. That was not the end of her troubles. Even though she could not eat well, she had gained weight and was suffering continuously from abdominal pain. Finally, she told me she must have an operation. I was told nothing more.

Mother took me to West Bromwich to stay with Uncle Joe and Auntie Gertie, who had offered to look after me. I felt very upset when Mother left but Auntie Gertie had promised that she would take me home and stay a few days when Mother came out of the nursing home. Aunt Gertie and Uncle Joe were very kind to me, although their grown-up daughters, Olive and Rachel, ignored me. However, there were dozens of books in the house and I could read undisturbed. It was easy to find a quiet corner where I could curl up with Bulldog Drummond.

The first night my bed was aired by a copper warming pan, much more exciting than a stone hot water bottle. I was allowed to read in bed, strictly against Mother's rules. The house and garden were magnificent and at my disposal. Uncle Joe and Auntie Gertie were happily married and never shouted at each other or anyone else. They treated me well. So why, I wondered, during those next two weeks, was I so miserable and lonely, missing my own mother and rumbustious, quick-tempered father?

I was surprised at myself. One incident did not help. I had been given permission to pick some flowers from the garden and I brought a bunch of red and white roses into my room. The maid, Maggie, shrieked when she saw them. 'Sure, but that's terribly unlucky, mixing red flowers with white. It brings death... your Mother will probably die now.' I cried my eyes out for a while then washed my face. I didn't want anyone to notice or ask me any questions, I felt so guilty.

Maggie was quite a character, as I found out on bath night. We were up in the one huge bathroom, with the large iron bath which took a tank of water to fill it. When I was clean, I hopped up and down in the water and told Maggie I needed to spend a penny and quickly. 'Oh, do it in the bath,' Maggie said and grinned. I only discovered why when Auntie Gertie called upstairs, 'Maggie! don't forget to keep Joan's bath water for Rachel.'

Mother wrote to Aunt Gertie and Uncle Joe with a note in the letter for me. She had only taken a rough, lined pad in to Denison Hall and Uncle Joe was most scathing about the cheap notepaper. For one disloyal second I could have murdered her for not using better paper but only for a second. I didn't care what the paper was like as long as Mother was getting better. When Auntie Gertie took me home, I was as delighted to see Mother as she was to have me back again. Dad was away so I carried my case upstairs myself. Inside, underneath my clothes, I found the letter Mother had sent to Aunt Gertie. There was no envelope, so without thinking, I read it.

'After the fibroids had been removed, despite the doctor's hope that everything would be all right, I went into labour. I had twelve hours hell, then miscarried. I've been told I mustn't have any more. At forty, I'm too old. It's been an awful time.'

I sat on the floor and cried for my mother, the baby and myself. Now I'd always be an only one. I wondered how the note had got into my case. Probably it was another of Maggie's little pranks.

Mother soon recovered enough for Aunt Gertie to go home and the household returned to what passed for us as normal. Mother banished Dad to the small bedroom at the end of the landing making his snoring the excuse. I tried to keep out of their way when the dinner or the furniture flew but at least I now had some friends to play with. When there were no adults around, we celebrated the approach of evening by taking a running jump at the street gas lamps which obliged by lighting up.

Dorothy had invited me to her birthday party. There were several children, including her little brother, Will, and their cousins from down the road. It was a very jolly affair. The highlight was provided by five-year old Will, who disappeared upstairs and forgot to come down. His mother sent me to find out what he was up to.

Will was starkers, balancing on one leg like a stork, paddling in the lavatory. His excuse was he'd lost sixpence. Why he'd taken all his clothes off, I never found out.

*

It was like old times, Mother walking with me to school. Harehills Lane was even steeper than Bayswater Road. I refrained from pointing out if I had gone to Brownhill in the first place, we should have saved our legs a lot of wear and tear. I was too frightened to chatter. As we passed Coldcotes Avenue, Mother gave a little shudder.

We walked through the school gates, in between laughing, shouting girls playing tig and enjoying their last moments of freedom before the bell went. Inside, Miss Swallow, the Headmistress, was waiting. She was a tall, full-bosomed lady, with white hair, a red face and a loud voice. Her eyes had a merry gleam which made her seem quite jolly but the glint was to prove more sarcastic than congenial.

Mother left me to it. I was taken into Miss Childe's classroom, which was large and high ceilinged, with half-tiled walls and green distemper. There were no pictures, only narrow high windows on the end wall. It was not beautiful but at least it was a proper schoolroom, seating about fifty girls. I was told to share a desk with Josie, who was tall and pretty.

While the register was called, I looked round as far as I dared at the other girls. My heart sank. They were all looking at me with equal interest and it was not hard to see why. They were wearing navy gymslips and black stockings. I was all in brown, the Priory colours. As the Brownhill uniform was not compulsory, Mother had not gone to the expense of re-fitting me and I stood out like a beacon. I also nervously studied Miss Childe. Was she the bit of a Tartar? She was tall, ramrod straight, with permed mid-brown hair, a wide smile, mocking eyes and the well developed calves of a dancer. She ran a successful dancing school in her spare time.

We started on some easy sums and I relaxed. This wasn't going to be too bad. Then Miss Childe loomed over me and inspected my answers. She informed me at the top of her voice that I should not henceforth be writing the figure two with a curly loop, and under no circumstances was the letter t to have the bar crossing the upright.

'We don't do sloppy writing here,' she said. This had my classmates straining to see what sort of a moron had arrived from Mars, who couldn't write a t and a 2 properly. Every time she approached, I quaked in case I was about to be pilloried. I bit my bottom lip for most of the lesson, only to have her poke fun at my expression, with an exaggerated imitation of me, which made the rest of the class think it was Christmas. I grew redder and redder as the morning wore on. She was a lot of a Tartar.

But when we were let loose at break, the girls were very friendly and I was included in a skipping game. They beat me hollow. Then it was back to the classroom. I braced myself for the mixture as before.

Miss Childe set us a composition on anything we had done in the holidays. I wrote about one of our picnics by the river at Ilkley when Dad had imitated a sheep so well, a lamb had responded by bleating round the side of the car, looking for its mother. Miss Childe mellowed after reading that and I breathed easier. It was obvious which subjects I should worry about. Every one except English.

Mother was delighted when I reassured her at lunch time that all my fellow pupils were clean and tidy, nicely spoken and well-behaved. The latter was guaranteed under Miss Childe! Yet she never used a cane, her tongue was enough.

I didn't tell Mother about Pauline, with her plump rosy cheeks and white mob cap, which she had removed to show me her pate, as bald as a pudding basin. 'I've had ring-worm for the second time,' she had confided, 'but I don't care. My hair used to be straight, but when it's been shaved, it grows back curly!' A stiff price to pay for curly hair, I thought. Now I understood Mother's warning, 'Don't borrow anyone else's comb or hat.'

In the afternoon, a young Jewish teacher, Miss Ochberg, took us for needlework. She was small, with large brown eyes, a soft voice and gentle manner. Everyone was devoted to her. She was incapable of drawing blood but controlled the class just as well. I learned to run-and-fell with minute stitches and, with a natural aptitude for sewing, managed to keep out of trouble for the rest of the afternoon.

I wondered if next morning would be as bad. It was worse. Miss Childe regarded me as a personal challenge. She was determined to drum the mysteries of basic maths into my head by either fair means or foul sarcasm. From the first lesson I was among her scholarship elite; two rows, to the right of the class. Miss Childe only concentrated on us, she barely looked at the others. But they didn't seem to mind, they were quite happy doing their sums at half our speed, whilst enjoying watching us squirm under her scathing jibes.

After several weeks, I could return her quick-fire mental arithmetic lobs with improved speed and accuracy. But she made it plain she expected much better than that. If I could only remember my tables and learn to count without using my fingers. I hid my waggling digits under the desk, well away from Miss Childe's eye. It was impossible to dodge her tongue for long but, although she embarrassed me, she didn't make me angry. I knew in my bones that despite her sarcasm, she was a magnificent teacher.

Mother renewed acquaintance with Mrs Howe, the newsagent's wife nearby and it was arranged I should lunch there every Tuesday. This gave Mother a chance to go to a cinema tradeshow with Mary. I looked forward to my weekly, unhurried lunch of beef and Yorkshire pud, especially when Mrs Howe was baking bread. She showed me how to fashion a bird, with currant eyes. When it was baked, I took it home. Mr Howe bred canaries, and Mother bought one which settled happily in our kitchen and sang for us for many years.

*

I was looking forward to Bonfire Night in our street. On Mischief Night, the night before, Dorothy and I were allowed to stay out until half past six, ringing our neighbours' doorbells then running away. It was fun going the rounds early before they realised they were being tricked. When we returned home, Dorothy found her front door knob was covered in treacle and tied to their dustbin lid. We wouldn't have dared do that and suspected the boys next door.

November the fifth was dry but cold. There was a patch of waste land two doors away where we were going to have the bonfire. Dorothy's family were fishmongers and provided a lorry-load of kipper boxes. Mother bought me some sparklers and Catherine wheels, and made a tray of delicious toffee. After tea, and muffled up to the ears, I ran out to join in. Mother came too, as did most of the parents and children in the street.

The bonfire blazed away, lighting the night air and burning the guy to a crisp. Rockets hovered above, raining down golden stars with a popping hiss while Catherine wheels spun whirls of colour on gate posts. I waved my sparklers around, keeping a wary eye on the boys at the same time in case they let off fire crackers near my legs. Bangers sounded off in the distance like gun fire. Dorothy's Mum brought out trays of jacket potatoes and parkin, then we finished off Mother's toffee. There was a wonderful smell of kippers, burnt wood, singeing wellington boots and spent fireworks. The flames were reflected in dirty smiling faces.

What a night! Only one thing spoiled it. Dorothy did not feel well, so went indoors early. The next day, she was ill, too ill for visitors.

'It's meningitis,' Mother said, looking at me, with worried eyes. I never saw my friend again. She died ten days later. The day after the funeral, her mother came over wheeling Dorothy's doll's pram, and gave it to me. How I had coveted that pram! But now that it was mine, I felt no pleasure, only sadness and guilt. I could not bear to play with it and decided I was too old for dolls.

Chapter Four

Behind Miss Swallow, who was taking assembly, there was a new, large poster exhorting us to clean our teeth every day. 'If you haven't any toothpaste,' it said, 'use soap and water.' I was pondering on the horrors of a mouthful of Lifebuoy, when Miss Swallow announced there would be two minutes silence in honour of Armistice Day. We stood, with heads bent, without any shuffling or a single whisper. The tension was too much for one girl, who burst into a peal of hysterical laughter. For once, there was no abrasive comment from the Headmistress.

After what seemed like an hour, we were sent to our classrooms. There, it was sprung on us that we were to have a medical examination, which appalled me as I did not relish the idea of getting undressed in front of any strange doctor. We were sent, two by two, into another room where one end was screened off. Finally, it was my turn to be examined.

Behind the screen, there was a lady doctor and a nurse, who wrote my name down while I undressed. 'Down to your knickers,' Nurse said. After I had struggled out of my gymslip, jumper, liberty bodice and knitted combinations, she started to laugh. 'Just look at this,' she nudged the doctor who was already gazing, fascinated at my chest. 'What on earth is it?'

'It' was my square of flannel, held on by a criss-cross of tapes, which Mother insisted I wear all the winter. The only time it came off, apart from in the summer, was when I had a bath. I had taken it for granted that everyone wore flannel on their chests but apparently in this tough part of the world Mother was a few years out of date. I was so mortified by the laughter that I swore I should never forgive her.

'A good job you don't live in the Dales,' the nurse grinned, 'or you'd have been sewn up for the winter with a rasher of bacon, fore and aft!' Mother would never have gone that far. Or would she? To crown it, there was a further indignity. 'You need your ears syringing,' the doctor said. On that I was dismissed with a red face and an appointment for the Children's Clinic. As I put all my layers back on again, I prayed no-one else had overheard the conversation.

Mother was not too pleased to hear I needed to attend the clinic; somehow it smacked of mismanagement, or worse, lack of hygiene. I felt vaguely ashamed, too, but was more interested in how soon I could get rid of my square of flannel. 'Not yet,' Mother was adamant. I just hoped I should not have to bare all again. As it turned out, this wasn't necessary, so I survived having my ears syringed and, as no-one accused Mother of neglect, she was mollified.

*

The next day, on my return from school, it was obvious from Mother's flushed face and bright eyes that she had forgotten her affront about my ears. 'Guess what!' she gasped, 'one of Dad's customers advertises in the Grand Theatre programmes, so he gets free tickets for most Monday nights. Can you believe it, he doesn't like the theatre, so he's giving the tickets to us!' I had seen *Peter Pan*, and was used to a yearly visit to the panto, but a weekly visit to the Grand! I had to sit down.

On the next Monday evening, I did my homework at the gallop. Then, without time to change, we were in the front dress circle enjoying the hubbub and air of expectancy before the curtain went up. I was intrigued by the binoculars which sixpence-in-the-slot would release from the backs of the seats; alas, Mother had brought her own. The lush crimson and gold Italianate decor and the lofty domed ceiling from which hung a spectacular chandelier were magnificent. The Grand Theatre certainly lived up to its name.

I settled down to watch the show, produced by the Leeds' Sylvians with much singing and dancing. This type of entertainment bored me but it made a pleasant change from reading, especially as our five-and-ninepenny seats had cost us nothing. Besides, during the interval, while Mother had a tray of coffee, I enjoyed an ice-cream served in a pretty glass dish.

My weekly visits did not materialise. Mother went with Jeanne or Mary to see the next few shows while I stayed at home and grappled with my sums. The dreaded scholarship exam was deemed more important than going to the theatre.

I hated staying in on my own, especially as we now had a telephone and answering it terrified me. There were benefits, however. Mother had found a stall in the market which sold packets of outdated magazines. As a treat the Girl's Own, Home Notes and Home Chat were left for me. Mother hid the more dubious Peg's Paper in the kitchen dresser but the minute she had gone out, I found it and read on.

I ignored the serials and short stories which were too sloppy to corrupt anyone, in favour of the Lonely Hearts column. This took a strictly moral tone towards all the problems submitted. 'To Worried Blue-Eyes: You must not consider seeing this man again, even if his wife does not understand him' and 'Anxious from Buxton' was exhorted, 'Under no circumstances must you ever do this again − if things turn out as you fear, confess to your mother.' 'Fed-up, Felixstowe' was told: 'Do not ignore your parents' warnings − staying out late with this boy is not advisable'. Finally, anyone under sixteen contemplating any mischief at all was urged to 'behave sensibly, and join the Girl Guides.'

After a time Mother relented and took me to see Zena Dare and Jack Melford in *Counsel's Opinion*. Mother had long been a fan of Zena Dare's, waxing lyrical about her glorious red hair. On stage, Miss Dare certainly looked beautiful but when she came out of the stage door, we saw a wrinkled, heavily made-up lady with dyed, crimped, ginger hair. I was totally disillusioned but Mother stayed loyal to her idol.

Not every theatre visit was memorable for the right reasons. One play was described in the programme as 'A tragedy of illicit love' and the heroine was an unmarried mother. Throughout the interval, Mother gave me sidelong glances whilst muttering into her tray of coffee, 'Most unsuitable, most unsuitable!'

On the Monday just before Christmas, the bookings for the pantomime were so bad that the manager rang Mother, begging her to bring twelve children. I raced up and down the street, gathering up my friends with halfpennies for their tram fares grasped safely in their gloves. Then Mother, like the Pied Piper, led us all upstairs to the front circle to see *Hop o'My Thumb*. Mona Vivian was the Principal Boy. I didn't mind so much that the Principal Boy was really a girl, if only they would not have so much singing, dancing and thigh-slapping holding up the story! Still, Mother was feeling generous and gave me half-a-crown for ices for us all so it was judged a rollicking good evening and a splendid start to the holidays.

*

'How about going to Miss Childe's dancing class?' Mother said, eyeing my puppy fat, 'it might trim you down a bit.' I thought it was a good idea, as Mother had recently taken me to see Pavlova and I rather fancied following in her footsteps. I was duly enrolled on Saturday morning.

There were dozens of girls there, standing in rows. Some wore their last year's Whitsuntide best: pink satin and frilly dresses. Others were in velvet with lace collars or ballet dresses. I only had a jumper and skirt. All wore white socks and dancing shoes. Mother had treated me to some pumps but drew the line at me casting my stockings in winter.

I was sent to the fourth row and as the pianist thumped out a movement from *The Nutcracker Suite*, we were taught the basic ballet foot positions. The girl in front of me was slim and pretty with rosy cheeks and bobbing ringlets. She was wearing real ballet shoes and could pirouette on her points, whereas I had difficulty turning my feet to the correct angle. My calves got in the way. As I watched her I was burning with envy and expected a lashing from Miss Childe's tongue but nothing happened. She was all smiles, and so pleasant to everyone, I thought I must be dreaming. As she was probably earning more each Saturday morning than she did teaching arithmetic all the week, her criticism was much more subtle. Week by week, I was moved further and further out of sight till I was on the back row.

Towards the end of the term, an announcement was made about the forthcoming dancing display. Ears stretched, I waited to see which part I should get. One by one, the names were called out, every one except mine. I hid my chagrin that I was not destined to be a prima ballerina and left. A further annoyance was that I had not whittled my shape down by a centimetre.

I had more success with elocution. I'd had lessons for some time and had passed all the exams except the last one, which I was far too young to take. 'What a pity,' Mother sighed. 'You'd have had letters after your name, and could have taught elocution when you were older'. It was not what I had in mind.

At the end of term, Miss Childe asked me to recite. I did my party piece: *Henri, ze performing flea.* I mimed Henri looping ze loop, with much rolling of the eyes, only to lose him a minute later. When he was found on a luckless stooge, he no longer looped ze loop, so he was put back there with, 'Alas! Zees is not Henri!'. As I dared to find the alien flea on Miss Childe, it brought the house down with the girls. I'd go on the stage as a career!

I stopped aspiring to the Old Vic when I grew thoroughly bored with learning set pieces and emoting *Hiawatha, Tosca,* and *Down by the Rio Grande.* As for the theory of elocution, none of it had improved my speech so I thought it a waste of time. The lessons continued as Mother had become firm friends with my teacher, Kitty. I liked her too. She was tall, elegant, well-spoken and charming. Then the lessons ended abruptly.

Mother had to give me some explanation and because she was so angry she told me the truth. 'Kitty has complained that your father went to her flat and tried to…press his attentions…' I gaped but was too stunned to say anything. Mother never mentioned it again and, oddly enough, cannot have used heavy artillery on Dad because the roof stayed on. I felt a pang for Mother, losing a friend. As for Kitty, it was unlikely she had consulted *Peg's Paper* where the advice would almost certainly have been, 'Never make mischief between man and wife'.

Apart from school work, I had other things on my mind, or rather, my chest. I was beginning to develop and was unprepared for it. In fact, I was horrified. One moment I had been as flat as a pancake, then almost overnight I was jiggling when I walked and bouncing when I ran. My liberty bodice wouldn't button and everything else felt tight. Mother never mentioned my burgeoning shape but she must have noticed it. When I finally ambushed her between the mangle and the sink and for the umpteenth time asked, 'How are babies born?' she went into the dining-room, unlocked her desk and produced a booklet entitled *What To Tell Your Daughter*, priced one-and-sixpence from *Home Notes*.

I sat down on the stool while she got on with her knitting. Her needles clicked as I read what was in store for me every month, when I should feel really grown-up. I couldn't wait! Then it became more precise. So I had a vagina, I stifled a giggle at that, it made me think of Victoria. The man's appendage, it seems, was a penis, that was news. But it was the next bit which had me reaching for the smelling salts. I could not believe it. Kissing and cuddling, yes. I knew that went on, I'd seen it at the cinema. But what a violation the rest of it sounded! What an intrusion! No wonder Mother wasn't too keen.

This clinical run-down did not mention love; gave no hint that a concerto might be played on the way. As for how a baby was born, it sounded as bad as Elsie's theory about the belly button. I looked at Mother's red face, buried in her knitting, counting her stitches. 'Does it hurt, having a baby?' I stammered.

'Well, it's soon forgotten,' she parried. Then swore me to secrecy. I was under no circumstances to discuss this booklet with any of my friends.

I promised. Excited and terrified by such heady information, but outwardly subdued, I looked in the shoe cupboard for my skipping rope and went out to play.

*

Mother had agreed to let me join the Girl Guides. There was a Jewish troop which met at Bransby Lodge on Chapeltown Road and when Mother left me there, she asked if anyone older could see me across Roundhay Road at hometime. A pretty, fair-haired girl called Iris, with smiling eyes and beautiful teeth, volunteered. When she did shepherd me across, we both chuckled as I was as big as she was.

I thoroughly enjoyed the meetings and sang Guide songs with gusto. I thought I had a lovely voice but whenever my parents heard me they laughed. Another illusion shattered! Round a campfire my voice passed muster. We bellowed *Itsy-whitsy spider, climbing up the spout* and *On Ilkley Moor bah t'at* until I was hoarse. Then to my astonishment, I was allowed to sing in the forthcoming Scout-Guide concert. Gertie and I performed *She sailed away, on a lovely summer's day, on the back of a crocodile*. Gertie's voice was about on a par with mine. No-one threw anything but I was never asked to sing anywhere again.

After the concert was over, I decided to try and qualify for a badge. Captain suggested housecraft. For this I had to produce a note from Mother, saying that I could lay and light a fire. As the only open fire we had was in the kitchen range which had a good down-draught and lit in a second, this was easy.

The idea of me becoming domesticated, appealed to Mother. 'It's about time, now you're eleven, that you helped me, instead of always having your nose in a book. You can dust the front room,' she snapped, throwing me the tail of one of Dad's old shirts. It was Sunday morning and I was outraged. I was half-way through *The Hound of the Baskervilles* and much preferred Sherlock Holmes to housework. Mother could knit and read at the same time but I knew I couldn't get away with dusting with a book in hand. I sulked off into the front room and approached the sideboard. It didn't look dusty to me. I scrunched the duster up, flicked it round the vase, candlesticks, silver tray, and then moved over to the mantelpiece. I navigated round the clock and two china vases, then returned the duster to the kitchen.

Mother's eyebrows shot up. 'You've been very quick!' Then she went into the front room to inspect. She picked up the vase on the sideboard, and hit the roof. 'You've only dusted round things. And what about the coffee table, underneath the sideboard and the window ledge?'

She was so annoyed I thought she might give me my first smack since I was three. 'It's your job to dust,' I yelled. 'It's your rotten furniture not mine!' Mother was so upset she rushed out of the room, nearly knocking Dad over as she passed him on the stairs. He came in to find me scowling.

'What on earth was that all about? You know, you must try and be kinder to your Mother, she's going through a trying time of life. It's very difficult for a woman.'

I opened my mouth to say 'Who's calling the kettle black?' but thought better of it. I stumped off to finish my book. Poor Mother with a bad-tempered husband and a child to match! She had to wait years for my apology.

She tried once or twice more to get me to dust but finally gave it up as a bad job. By accident I had discovered that if you do a chore badly enough, you don't get asked again!

The Saturday morning came when I was to be tested for my housecraft badge. I walked in with a show of confidence I didn't feel. 'Sit down,' the examiner said. Her uniform looked impressive but her smile was kind. The first question was, 'How would you clean your living room?'

I racked my brains. 'Oh,' I said, playing for time, 'I'd dust everywhere thoroughly, taking care to go under all the ornaments, then vacuum the carpet.' I looked her in the eye and hoped my neck wasn't red from shame.

She seemed satisfied and then asked, 'How would you go about doing the weekly wash?'

Oh crikey, Mother did the washing at six-thirty in the morning when normal people were asleep. On a fine summer's day the ironing was done before breakfast. I vaguely knew everything had to be mangled but not much else. 'Well,' I said, 'firstly...' I was getting desperate. '...I'd strip the kitchen for action.'

She was smiling encouragement. 'Then?'

I had a sudden flash of inspiration. 'Then I'd read the instructions on the packet of washing powder!' The Guider gave me my badge, whether for housecraft or chutzpah, she didn't say.

A housecraft badge was one thing but there was no chance of me waffling my way through the scholarship exam and I grew colder as the day drew near. Miss Childe had drilled me non-stop in arithmetic and I was now much quicker than I had been but that wasn't saying much. The other girls had been thoroughly taught for years. I had only been there for a few months. I had worked like a beaver but without any natural aptitude for maths. All I could do when March approached was keep my fingers crossed and do my best.

We sat the exam in our school with an invigilator present. I took a deep breath and tackled the sums first. As usual the problems were my biggest hurdle. One was a stinker, about two men setting off for work at different times, at different speeds, and at what stage in their journey did they meet? Later when we compared notes, I found Josie, Marjorie, Anne and the others had arrived at one answer and I had given another. What if all mine were wrong? I put my trust in the English paper.

It seemed a long time to wait for the results in June. I had to try and put it out of my mind which was difficult. This was my last chance.

*

I walked home from school, feeling hot and sticky. It was a mild day for March but I was still in my winter woollies, complete with chest protector and lisle stockings of a particularly virulent shade of khaki. By now everyone else in my class was wearing knee-length socks so I was hoping that Mother would relent and allow me to cast a clout before May was out. 'Don't be so ridiculous!' she said as I dumped my schoolbag in the kitchen.

After tea Mother said she was going out for half-an-hour. While I had the house to myself, I went into the small front bedroom where Mother kept all her sewing tackle. Apart from the sewing machine, there was a small chest of drawers housing tacking thread, a full range of Sylkos and various types of scissors including a pair shaped like a stork. I peeled off my stockings, seized a pair of shears and cut the baggy tops off at the knee. After a neat bit of herring-bone stitching and a twist of my garters I had a pair of three-quarter socks. When Mother came home I was sitting down with my gymslip covering my knees so she never noticed a thing.

The next morning before we started our lessons, I nonchalantly showed Josie my bare knees. 'I've got three-quarter socks on like you,' I said.

'Don't be so daft!' she laughed. 'You've chopped tops off your stockings – anyone can see that!' Then she got on with her sums, leaving me cut down to the size of my socks.

That evening Mother and I went next door to see Alice and Jack, who had recently moved in with Mary, Jack's daughter by his first marriage. Mother had become friendly with Alice, who was a small, well-spoken woman in her forties, with large protruding eyes which could suddenly go blank and make her as inscrutable as any sphinx. I found this a bit offputting but Mother didn't seem to notice. Alice was in the middle of serving tea and

I was delighted as she made delicious buns. Mother was very happy to eat anyone else's baking but never did any herself. 'Too fattening', she said. It was jolly, sitting in their kitchen, scoffing buns and drinking tea. Mary, a big, raw-boned girl in her early twenties, with full lips, a pudding-basin haircut, and eyes bright with temper, was doing all the washing-up. Everything, once washed and drained, had to be wiped with a clean, dry dish cloth, then inspected by Alice before it could be touched by the tea towel. I was glad Mother wasn't as fussy.

Jack, heavily built and quiet, was buried behind the evening paper. He had come to Leeds hoping to get a job in one of the tailoring factories, preferably Burton's. Montague Burton had recently built a modern factory and taken tailoring out of the dark ages of sweatshops. So far, Jack had had no luck as there was no shortage of tailoring skills in Leeds.

When Dad came home on Friday night, Mother mentioned Jack's difficulty in finding a job. Dad looked up from his paper. 'Jack seems a decent sort! I'll ask Louis when I play cards with him over the weekend.' Louis was an executive at Burton's. True to his word, Dad asked his friend to do his best for Jack and a good job was found for him in the cutting room.

Alice and Mother were now even closer. Mother ignored the hostility between Alice and her stepdaughter Mary. It was not her business. It did, however, provide us with some entertainment. The curtain went up every morning at seven-thirty when Mary, with a carpet beater shaped like a tennis racket, was sent out into the drive to beat the rugs. Mother would call me to listen.

'The quality' . . thump . . thump . . 'of mercy' . . thwack . . thwack . . 'is not strained' . . thump . . thump. . . 'It droppeth like the gentle rain . .' A pause, then 'from heaven' was accompanied by an even more murderous swipe. Her face was suffused with temper and she obviously would have preferred to have used the beater for some other purpose. Every day she treated us to the same piece which sorely tried Mother's patience until eventually she exclaimed, 'Why can't she give us a bit of *Hamlet* for a change!'

*

There was great excitement when Mother and Dad received an invitation to Uncle Lewin's birthday party in Birmingham. They wanted to go but it meant spending the night there and leaving me behind. Alice offered to have me and Mother accepted. It was convenient and Mother trusted her.

Alice showed me into the small guest room, which was sterile-clean and chilly. Then Alice offered to show me something else. She took me into her room and opened a double wardrobe. It was choc-a-bloc with brand new dresses and suits, tacking threads still in their pleats, all shrouded in tissue paper. Proudly she showed me the labels; Marshall and Snelgrove's, Schofield's, Matthias Robinson, Brown Muff's. I was staggered. Mother's clothes were not in the same class; she could never have afforded them. Alice stroked the dresses, caressing the silks. Her pale eyes showed no emotion.

We went downstairs. 'I think we'll go to town,' Alice said, reaching for her shopping basket. She had on the only suit we had ever seen her wear, a loud brown and green check usually topped by a mangy ginger fox. Today was mild so she left the fur on the hall stand. I wondered, as we waited for a tram, when Alice would appear in her finery. Then the neighbours' eyes would pop.

Our first stop was at Woolworth's. I loved wandering round the stalls and looking at the small dolls. I sighed. I needed a brassiere more but decided to leave it for another week as the store was crowded and stifling. Alice had bought nothing. 'Shall we go?' she said over her shoulder as we elbowed our way towards the door.

Then I noticed it and froze. There was an unwrapped jar of Pond's cold cream in Alice's basket. 'Look at that!' I gasped. There were two spots of colour in Alice's cheeks and a gleam of excitement in her eyes before they blanked into their usual inscrutability.

'I wonder how that got there,' she murmured, looking straight at me. 'Did you put it there?'

I shook my head in horror. 'Well, perhaps it fell in?' Alice said, standing, making no move. I was shaking but gathered what was left of my wits and babbled that we had better put it back from where it had 'fallen.'

Taking no chances I struggled through the crowd to the cosmetics counter and, having snatched the jar from her basket, put it back. I did not breathe freely until we were well clear of Woolworth's. I had convinced Alice I felt sick so fortunately she had not suggested going into any other shops. Once on the tram, I was still so upset that my usual prattle was stilled and I pretended to be engrossed by the huge excavation in Briggate where the foundations for Lewis's were being laid. Alice's colour was high and her lips pursed into a fixed smile all the way home.

Back in Copgrove Road, for once I ate little lunch and made an excuse that I had homework to do so that I could stay upstairs in the bedroom. The downstairs rooms, apart from the kitchen, were kept dust-sheeted and locked.

I went down at tea-time as I was both hungry and cold but Alice's buns had lost their flavour. I had a book to read so I went to bed early and I was just dropping off to sleep when I heard Jack and Alice coming to bed. It was not long before they had settled down. Then I nearly fell out of bed. Loud, wet, smacking noises were coming from the main bedroom. Jack was kissing Alice as noisily as his daughter beat the rugs. He sounded like an energetic sink plunger. There were accompanying whispers of endearment coming round the open door. I supposed it was better than living with constant warfare but I wasn't too sure. It had been a very peculiar day.

*

Next day Mother came home delighted with her visit to Birmingham. Uncle Lewin had celebrated his birthday not only by hosting a dinner party but also by giving each of his nieces and nephews seventy pounds, one for every year he had lived. Our summer holiday was now assured.

Mother told me all about the party. They had been regaled with a nine course dinner at the Assembly Rooms complete with orchestra and cabaret. The speeches had been excellent but the gossip had been even better. Aunty Rae-from-Torquay was still sporting an outrageous ginger wig, consorting with an elegant gentleman friend without the benefit of clergy and not speaking to Aunty Rae-from-Birmingham.

Unfortunately, a waiter had spilled tomato soup into Dad's lap. Mother had fully expected a scene but Dad was so busy entertaining his fellow guests from his fund of jokes, he had mopped himself down and never said a word. 'Typical!' Mother snorted. 'He can blow up over nothing at all but confounds me by not saying a word when I most expect it!'

I had no chance to talk to Mother about the strange goings-on next door as Alice had come round. I was sent to bed early because I had to go to school in the morning. My stomach was in a knot as the scholarship results were expected.

There was an air of excitement in the classroom. Miss Childe, her complexion more florid than usual, was smiling as she removed a sheet of paper from an envelope.

I hardly dared breathe as she came over to our section where for months I had been chivvied and mocked in a welter of arithmetic. I should soon find out whether our joint efforts had paid off.

Miss Childe started reading out the list of passes as the rest of the class sat back and listened with a mixture of envy and indifference. She came to the end. All the names were called except mine. This was far worse than not being in the dancing display. This was horrible. Then she turned to me and said, 'Oh! Joan Ogus. You are a borderline case and have to go to Roundhay High School and sit for a further entrance examination, then have an interview with the Head Mistress.'

A borderline case! It sounded as if I weren't 'all there' but at least it was better than outright failure. I went home at teatime and told Mother. She looked upset. We were both subdued for the rest of the evening.

The day before the interview, Miss Childe called me over for a final briefing. 'Tomorrow, for the interview, wear your glasses,' she said. I was astonished as I only wore my specs for reading and classwork.

'Your glasses will make you look more intelligent,' she explained and then did something unusual for her — she smiled and said, 'Good luck!'

I hardly slept that night. I'd worked so hard but obviously hadn't caught up so what chance did I have of scraping through yet another foul arithmetic paper? I finally dropped off to sleep after saying my tables forwards, backwards and sideways.

The next afternoon I walked up to Roundhay High School, wearing my best green coat, matching stitched beret and my tortoise-shell rimmed glasses. The ground seemed to come up and meet me. I prayed I should not trip up and spoil my intellectual image.

The school was new and huge and set in grounds which seemed like a park compared with Brownhill's concrete yard. On arrival I was taken into a classroom large enough for thirty girls. There were no horrible lavatory-tiled walls but cream paint and big windows overlooking the tennis courts. I was relieved that there were some other girls there and I was not the only semi-failure.

We took off our coats and hats, sat down at the desks and read through the papers. Then I carefully dipped my pen into the inkwell and tackled the sums. They didn't seem too difficult but I didn't trust my judgement on arithmetic. I only hoped my composition on Bonfire Night might impress. After the papers had been gathered in, we had about half an hour to wait. Then we were called in, one at a time, to Miss Vyvyan's study.

I opened her study door with clammy hands. The room was light with a desk slanting across the bay window. I was dazzled by the spring sunshine and Miss Vyvyan, who was sitting there, wearing her gown with an air of authority. She was the founder of the school and looked formidable. Her grey hair was fastened back into a bun from which a few wisps had dared to escape. Her fine grey eyes were transfixed by the paper I had just completed. She frowned down her aquiline nose at me. I still had my glasses on but it was hard trying to look clever when I was shaking.

'Tell me, child, what is thirty plus one?'

'Forty,' I answered promptly. I hadn't been schooled in speedy mental arithmetic for nothing. Miss Vyvyan looked as if she were about to explode.

'Thirty, plus one, child!'

My mind went blank. What was wrong with my answer? Then the enormity of my mistake hit me. I stammered out 'Thirty-one!' wrapped in an apology. I wanted to curl up and die. This would definitely have finished off my chances. I conceded, in that split second, that I was indeed well over the borderline towards idiocy. Miss Vyvyan looked sternly at me. 'You really have been a very careless gel.'

Had I not been so mortified, I should have seen a gleam of amusement behind her grey eyes as she continued, 'I trust that if I accept you as a pupil here, you will take more care in the future!'

The composition about Dad bringing home some larger-than-usual sparklers, guaranteed safe for indoor use but which then burnt holes in the carpet, might have clinched it. Or it could even have been my glasses. But whatever the reason, I'd crossed the borderline. I had my scholarship. I was going to a high school, to this high school! I sang all the way home, rejoicing. Miss Childe was equally delighted that I hadn't spoiled her success rate.

On Saturday Dad gave me a mammoth treat. He took Mother and me to see Maurice Chevalier and Claudette Colbert in *The Smiling Lieutenant* at the newly opened Paramount in the Headrow. We had not been there before as it was half-a-crown to go in, compared with ninepence at the other cinemas.

The cinema was all green and gold with a lush, deep-pile carpet. Besides the film, which was a smash hit, there was a song-and-dance stage spectacular. Dad never turned a hair at the expense nor shouted at Mother once during the outing. As for me, I was so happy I did not want the evening to end.

Chapter Five

There were new neighbours next door to Alice and Jack. Mrs Hill was slim and pretty, with a lot of pillar-box red lipstick, light brown hair and a Clara Bow kiss curl pressed on to her forehead. She had been on the stage. 'Musical comedy, darling,' she told Mother. She certainly had the shapely legs of a dancer and a theatrical way of speaking, emphasising her remarks with a wave of her cigarette holder. She blew perfect smoke rings.

All the neighbours were told, 'Our best furniture is away being repolished. The carpets have gone to be cleaned and the curtains..remade...' No more furniture ever turned up and when we were finally invited over the doorstep, there were only three chairs and a rug in the back room. The front room was furnished with a crate of beer and a piano, on which Mr Hill, a good looking man with a Ronald Colman moustache and patent leather hair, could play any tune by ear.

Mrs Hill, who had a good soprano voice, leaned against the piano and gave a good impersonation of Gertrude Lawrence in revue. She also knew all Mother's favourites from *The Maid of the Mountains* and *The Desert Song*. We couldn't have cared less about the lack of furniture, we had such fun with the sing-song. I was sorry Dad was away and missing it all. When Mrs Hill heard I had suffered from chilblains, she told me, 'Darling, you must bathe them in urine. It's so good for chilblains!' I decided the cure sounded worse than the ailment.

On my way to school in the mornings, I saw Mrs Hill in a fetching nightie lean out of her bedroom window to blow kisses to her departing husband. They certainly brought a touch of colour to the street.

I was really most unobservant for I never noticed Mrs Hill growing fatter. So I was quite surprised, later that summer, when I was passing by on my way home from Brownhill, to hear the most dreadful moaning coming through Mrs Hill's open bedroom window. I ran in to Mother and gasped, 'I think Mrs Hill must be terribly ill. She's moaning and groaning.'

I couldn't understand why Mother started to laugh.

'She'll get worse before she gets better!' Before I could ask any more questions, Alice called across the drive to say that Mrs Hill had given birth to a fine baby boy.

I then understood what had been happening. 'But why all the moaning,' I asked Mother. 'Does it hurt so much?'

Mother gazed sentimentally into space and said, 'You forget the pain the moment you hold the baby in your arms.' I wondered why she wasn't looking me in the eye.

When we called to see Mrs Hill and the baby with some bootees Mother had knitted, we were fascinated by her line in baby talk.

'Billy-bo, come to Mummy-bo and have your bottle-bo, then I'll change your nappy-bo and wipe your botty-bo!' It was as entertaining as her singing.

After a time I realised that Mrs Hill seemed to know more about curing chilblains than looking after the baby. He spent day and night in his pram in the kitchen amongst unwashed nappies hung to dry over the oven door. The oven provided the only heat. But Billy thrived amongst the gas fumes and cigarette smoke although he was pale and cried whenever he saw a strange face.

But soon the neighbours were agog over something else; Mr Denvers, the greengrocer, who plied his trade up and down our street with a large horse and cart. He was an amiable man with a cheeky grin and a red kerchief knotted round his neck. His brand of lip and quality greens must have charmed Mrs Hill for despite the kisses still blown to her husband at eight-thirty each day, Mr

Denvers' horse was to be found impatiently pawing the ground outside the Hills' house for hours on end.

I couldn't understand what there was for Mother to laugh about, or what would be entertaining for Mr Denvers, listening to Mrs Hill talking 'Billy-bo' nonsense to the baby through a pall of cigarette smoke.

One day, when I was playing up the street, a lady was seen to arrive at the Hills', while Mr Denver's horse was outside neighing for Mr Denvers. It was Mrs Denvers. Whatever went on inside the house was never revealed but Mr Denvers never came up our street again, much to Mother's annoyance. 'Why he had to make a fool of himself, and deprive us of his services, I can't imagine. Men!'

No-one cold-shouldered Mrs Hill. She seemed harmless enough as far as we were concerned. But she told one whopper too many to Mrs Marshall opposite, claiming that Mother had borrowed a pound from her and had not repaid it. As Mother was very thrifty, and had never borrowed any money from anyone, she was furious. We kept clear of Mrs Hill after that. I was really sorry she had blotted her copy book, she was such a lively character. Not long afterwards the Hills did a moonlight flit. There were only crates of empties left to show they had ever lived there.

*

In the summer Mother made arrangements to take me to Bridlington for a month before I started at Roundhay in September. To my delight it was decided that Mary, Alf and Henry were to come with us for the first week.

The day of our departure was cold, damp and misty so Mother made me wear my leather coat and wellington boots to save room in the trunk.

'What's in it, bricks?' Dad grumbled, as he strapped it

behind the car. Mother had filled every corner with food as well as taking a carrier bag of her homemade ginger wine. Dad was in a foul mood as he hated driving at the weekend. He was not having a holiday so would also have to face the return journey.

After Mother had locked up the house she had to go back inside as she'd forgotten the canary. Dad yelled as she carried the birdcage out, 'Just like a woman – always forgetting something!' Then he reversed down the drive and there was a sickening crunch as steel bulldozed iron. He had forgotten to open the garden gates. However, he soon recovered his good humour and as we drove along the country roads, we had a fine old time singing *Daisy* and *There Ain't No Sense, Sitting On The Fence*. Henry and I giggled away, squashed like sardines in the back seat with Mother and Mary. By now the sun had come out from behind the mist and I was regretting my leather coat and boots. We were all making so much noise no one noticed a road sign at the bottom of the hill, showing a sharp incline. We were starting to climb Garrowby Hill.

'This seems to be a bit steep,' said Dad as he tried, too late, to change into bottom gear. The car, daunted by the looming hill, was bucking like an overladen bronco. The engine sputtered, coughed and died. Smoke was coming out of the radiator. 'Oh Lord!' muttered Dad, 'I'm sorry but all of you in the back will have to get out and start walking. Alf and I will coast down to the bottom of the hill till I get the engine going.'

I couldn't bear to watch Dad reversing back down again. Mary wasn't too pleased to see the car disappearing either as hiking was especially hard for her because of her limp. The only one who was enjoying the adventure was Henry, who found a stone to scuff uphill and pretended he was playing football. By now it was sweltering. I took off my coat but carrying it made me even hotter. There had been no time to leave it in the car.

For half-an-hour we slogged up the hill. The only noise was our heavy breathing and the sound of birds cawing overhead. Suddenly, way behind us, there was a honking and tooting as our chariot came into view. 'At last,' gasped Mother, as we paused at the side of the road, ready to leap aboard at the first sign of braking.

With a cheery wave from Alf but not even a nod from Dad who was holding grimly on to the wheel as if welded to it, they passed us by.

'Of all the cheek! Your Father takes the biscuit!' Mother was furious.

When our party had finally trailed over the brow of the hill and tottered on to the straight, we found Dad and Alf sitting under a tree by the roadside with their jackets off and ties loosened. They had their eyes closed and were each licking a large ice-cream cornet. The ice-cream vendor was nowhere to be seen.

'Why the devil didn't you stop for us?' Mother demanded.

'I didn't dare or I might not have got her started again,' Dad said between licks. He kept quiet that the sign at the bottom of Garrowby Hill had warned, 'Change into bottom gear NOW!'

Four hours after setting off, we rounded a corner and..magic moment! there was the sea. I longed for a bathe but knew I should have to spend a day getting acclimatised before I was allowed to get wet. Soon we were outside Mrs Nelson's terraced house in Tennyson Avenue. The doorstep was step-stoned, the paint sparkled and there was an aspidistra in the dining-room window.

'It's reasonable at four-and-sixpence a night. Of course the use of the cruet is extra,' Mother told me with a smile. The northern foible of charging for the salt and pepper always amused her.

Mother inspected our room. The brass bed with a

heavy white cotton fringed bedspread, passed muster, also the washstand with jug and basin. There was a chamberpot under the bed. Ellen, the maid, would come round every morning with hot water for washing or shaving, and later had the unenviable job of emptying the slops. As the house was full, I wondered where she slept. I soon found out. She spent her nights on a door on top of the bath. The tips must have made it worthwhile. I knew from last year that Mother would give her half-a-crown at the end of the month and embarrass me by saying, 'Buy yourself a grand piano!'

After a walk along the prom we had a meal in the Lounge Cafe, then Dad had to set off for home. The rest of us ambled round the harbour until the grown-ups decided that we'd turn in early.

By ten o'clock Mother and I were in bed, fast asleep, when suddenly there was the noise of a gunshot in the bedroom. I was terrified. Mother stifled a scream as she sat up, her pink vanity net askew. She groped for the light. There was no-one there apart from Dicky, our canary, squawking under his cover.

Then we saw it — a cork, embedded in the ceiling. 'Oh crumbs!' Mother gasped, 'it's my ginger wine!' It had blown up. 'I hope they won't charge me,' Mother murmured, as she settled down again. 'Don't say anything to Mrs Nelson. What she doesn't know about, won't grieve her.'

The next morning, Henry and I wandered round the main square near the harbour. We were lured by the music from Harold Fielding's open-fronted shop, where the walls were festooned with sheet music, and a pianist was entertaining a crowd by thumping out the latest hits. We joined in with *You Are My Heart's Delight* and *I'll See You Again*. It was great fun and no-one told me to keep quiet or I'd make it rain.

A fishy smell from the quay and the winkle stall hung

in the air. At the end of the jetty, a salesman was singing the praises of a huge waterless cooker. Mother had been tempted until she realised she would need an extra cupboard to go with it. Henry preferred pressing his nose to the window of the rock shop, watching a huge pink skein being pulled and twisted by hand into a stick of rock with Bridlington down the middle.

We meandered down to the beach which was teeming with people. Most of the little girls were in bridesmaids' bonnets and pink satin frills tucked into their knickers. Their dads wore knotted hankies on their heads and had taken off their starched collars. Mothers were trying to relax while keeping anxious eyes on children paddling. One family leaning against the promenade wall caught my eye. The mother was breastfeeding the baby, then after passing him over to her husband, she offered her ample breast to her three-year-old, standing next in line. I was so astonished, I stood and gawped. "Appen she fancies a drop, an' all,' said the father, grinning at me. I fled.

I caught up with Henry and we bought a halfpenny cornet each, then stayed at the kiosk to watch ice-cream sandwiches being made with a deft little gadget which flicked them up. This was more entertaining than the Bing Boys, who had their own stage on the sands and a corny line in old jokes. We found our folks on the beach just in time to hear Mother say she intended to have a dip the next day before breakfast. My mouth dropped. She explained, 'I'm far too big to bathe in front of other people. I only dare go in early in the day when there's hardly anyone around. We'll start tomorrow first thing.' Henry volunteered to join us and to my surprise Mary agreed.

At seven-thirty the next morning it was misty and bleak when we walked briskly up Tennyson Avenue. The houses all looked asleep with most of the curtains drawn.

Only the milkman was about. Mother and I both had on our home-made striped towelling robes over our swim suits. Mine was hand-knitted in brown and beige stripes. Mother's was a heavy navy cotton with short sleeves and a blue-edged skirt down to her knees. She had a rubber mob cap to protect her hair and I had a regulation helmet. Henry wore a black one-piece costume with holes cut out of the sides beneath his raincoat. He carried his clothes wrapped in a towel under his arm.

We were warm from the walk until we dropped our coats on the beach. Although the sky was grey and a sharp wind was whistling round our shoulders, there was something special about being up and about so early. The newly washed sand bore no foot marks. There were only half a dozen other foolhardy characters sharing the beach and they were in the distance. One was a gentleman with only one leg, who had to drag himself along to reach the sea; another was a middle-aged woman wearing a backless navy swimsuit over a deep white brassiere.

The three of us entered the water gingerly. We were honour-bound to get wet all over. Mother had never learnt to swim but enjoyed a splash around in shallow water while Henry and I breaststroked for a few yards. I nudged Henry. 'Let's duck Mother!' and we made towards her and pushed her over on to her back.

She went under the water and we laughed. Her waterlogged costume and girth combined to hold her under. She was floundering and could not get up.

Then suddenly it was unfunny. Mother was drowning. Henry and I both lunged forward and pulled at her arms but she was too heavy for us and her shoulders slid from our grasp. I was frantic.

By a combined superhuman effort Mother hung on to us both and managed to roll over and we heaved her upright. She coughed and spluttered for what seemed an eternity before she got the sea out of her lungs and started to breathe normally again. Her face was swollen and red from the effort and she looked grim.

She said nothing to Henry, only addressed me slowly. 'Don't ever do anything like that again. Ever.' I felt more contrite than if she had been angry. She looked sad and dignified. The innocent jaunt was ruined. I mumbled an apology. Chastened into silence, we went back for our coats. Mother dried Henry down and helped him to get dressed.

We all three livened up after a mug of cocoa apiece from the stall on the promenade. We were now glowing and I knew from the way Mother held my hand all the way up Tennyson Avenue that she had forgiven me. But I had not forgiven myself.

*

Dad came to see us on the following Friday, with the intention of staying until Monday morning and calling on customers on the way home. The car was parked in a nearby garage, its rails of clothes discreetly hidden behind the grey curtain Mother had made. Dad was obviously pleased to be with us. He relished the sea air and told me, while we were deep-breathing along the promenade, that he was thirteen before he ever saw the sea. 'And that was only for a day on a Jews' Free School trip.'

He sounded bitter and Mother's lukewarm welcome hadn't helped. He was banished to the attic at Mrs Nelson's. Mother had not volunteered that I should go instead of him. I could have shaken her and was feeling grumpy when we were at breakfast despite the beautiful year-old baby whose parents let me feed her. I had stopped playing with dolls but a real live baby, that was different! I felt strange and at odds with myself. I had grown, and felt self-conscious in my short dresses. Every shop window reflected my changing shape.

Mother had gone to the pier to buy our lunch for Mrs Nelson to cook. We ate boiled dabs, all bones and no flesh, every day for two weeks, while some of the other guests on full board enjoyed roast beef and Yorkshire pudding. It was tantalising. But I didn't dare complain as I was not too popular with Mother or Mrs Nelson after yesterday's debacle over the salad. Just as I was about to put some lettuce on my fork something moved. A whopping caterpillar looked up at me. I let out a yell and announced the news in a voice which could have been heard at Flamborough Head. Mrs Nelson had nearly thrown us out. What was worse Mother had made me apologise to Mrs Nelson as if it were all my fault!

While Mother was shopping, Dad and I boarded a fishing coble. The sea had looked calm inshore but soon the boat was going up and down like a rollercoaster. There was a horrible smell of diesel fuel and before long I felt so ill I wanted to die. I caught nothing but Dad fared better. As we climbed back on to dry land, he was proudly carrying a bunch of undersized dabs.

Saturday was Carnival Day at the Spa and Mother improvised a fancy dress for me from brown paper and string. I was togged out as a brown paper parcel. I walked through the town to the Spa, trying to look nonchalant, as if brown paper were my normal dress.

The first event was in the open air: an adult egg-and-spoon race. Dad entered, clowning with a hop-skip-and a jump until he tripped himself up and sprawled headlong onto the concrete. Instead of rushing to help him up, I stood there curdled with embarrassment. Why couldn't I have a normal, quiet, self-effacing, humdrum father, preferably one with a serene temper who would suit Mother? Fortunately, the Knobbly Knees competition, held in the concert hall, gave him an opportunity to show off outrageously without doing himself a mischief. He ballet-danced on to the stage, pirouetted with his trousers rolled up and offered a chorus from *Pagliacci* for good measure. Mother muttered 'Silly fool!' but the audience loved it, and he received a great round of applause, but no prize for his knees.

Then it was my turn to go on with the pirates, fairies, Demon Kings and gypsies for the fancy dress line-up. The fairy looked lovely and my eye turned green, but, to my delight, when the compere held his hand over my head there was a good round of applause. Mother's ingenuity gained me the third prize, a ten shilling voucher from a fancy-goods' shop. It would buy me a leather purse and a penknife.

I stood in the wings for Mother to remove the paper and had to wait patiently while she undid the string. Wasting string was unknown in our house. She had just unravelled the final knot when the Prettiest Bathing Belle competition was announced.

'How about entering that?' Mother teased and for devilment, before she could say 'Stop!' I ran on to the stage. When I saw how pretty some of the grown-up girls were, I regretted my cheek. They all looked quite glamorous in smart beach trousers, and one or two even had matching hats. Why had I been such an idiot! There was only one thing for it: smile, and hope I wasn't booed off.

The compere walked behind us. A hand over the shapely blonde's Marcel waves and all the men clapped and stamped. There was a lovely brunette with lots of lipstick and a figure as good as Joan Crawford's. Thunderous clapping greeted her. I knew Dad would be rooting for the redhead; he always joked he liked 'carrots.' Polite ripples saluted the rest of the entrants and then it was my turn. The compere's hand was over my dark hair, brown face, nondescript aertex blouse, harlequin-bright homemade shorts and plump legs which the uncles all loved to pinch.

I smiled bravely and a ripple of amusement went round, followed by a roar of approval. The mums in the audience, bless them, preferred a chubby twelve-year-old to the glamour pusses their husbands were drooling over. They clapped and shouted for me better than any claque! To my astonishment, Dad's amusement and Mother's delight, I came second. That was my only beauty competition. I never pushed my luck again.

Dad's pleasant weekend was shortlived. At tea-time, back at the 'digs', a man was waiting from the garage to say there had been a burglary, our car had been rifled and all the stock had gone. Dad left for home right away. He looked haggard, his jaws clamped on to his pipe. Although his dark hair was still nearly as thick as ever, he looked nearer fifty than thirty-eight as he kissed me goodbye.

That evening, Mother and I went back to the Spa to sit in the balcony watching the dancing. I jiggled my toes as the couples swirled and dipped, tails flying and dresses twirling. The colours and the music made me long to join in. I too wanted longer skirts, grown-up fashions. I was fed up with childish things.

Most evenings, Mother patronised the fruit machines and roll-the-penny-on-to-the-squares in the amusement arcades on the front while I won bars of stick-jaw toffee by catching ping-pong balls in a fishing net. The What-the-butler-saw-machines were taboo when Mother was around so I waited for a peek until she had gone for a drink in the Lounge. All I eventually saw was a woman in an Edwardian outfit undress down to her laced-up stays. I hooted. What a waste of a penny! That decided me. I'd had enough of Bridlington, dabs, and Mother, who was determined to have a last early dip the next day despite the chill in the air.

We went down, only to find the tide was in almost to the sea wall and the sea looked too choppy for bathing. We stood on the strip of beach, watching the boats and their skippers waiting for customers. The beach shelved near where we were standing and the waves were walloping against the boats. A thin little boy, who was paddling nearby, was caught offguard by an incoming ferocious wave which knocked him over and sucked him under the water.

A boatman saw what was happening and leapt in as fast as his thigh boots allowed. The sea went right over the tops and he was soaked but he managed to grab the child, who was brought out like a half-drowned rag doll, blue, with chattering teeth and rattling limbs. He was sick and looked pathetic.

Mother ministered hot cocoa from the kiosk to both of them. The sailor thanked her as we hovered round the child, who still looked terrible. As suddenly as the wave had materialised, a rat-faced woman appeared, claiming the child with, 'You little nuisance! Take me eyes off you for a second and you get wet all over.'

'He nearly drowned,' Mother said to mollify her and indicated the seaman. 'This gentleman saved him and got soaked too.'

She was wasting her breath. The woman grabbed the boy by his arm and marched off without turning her head. Mother was incensed. All the way back for breakfast she held my hand so hard it hurt, as if the sea might leap over the promenade and grab me too. I realised if I had been in that child's place, Mother would not have been indifferent. I squeezed her hand back again. The next day, the sun came out, a real scorcher.

'Here, you've forgotten your bucket and spade,' Mother called after me, as we set off for the beach. 'Oh, I'm too old for kids' games,' I snapped but took them from her with a shrug. We walked up the avenue in silence. I was in a dream world where there was no place for Mother.

We sat down on the beach and I said I was going for a swim. The sea was lovely, clean and warm as I waded out until it was deep enough for me to swim. There were plenty of people in the water but no-one near until a man bobbed up right in front of me. He was in his thirties, tall and powerfully built.

'Hullo,' he said and as I stood up, he lunged. Before I could back away, he had put two large hands under my armpits, gripped me tightly, and lifted me out of the water, bouncing me up and down. I was powerless. His eyes were glassy, riveted to the shape under my bathing suit, while he muttered, 'You little beauty, you little beauty.'

Fear churned my stomach. This was something outside my ken, nasty, smelling of danger. I acted instinctively, doubled my legs up at right angles to my body and kicked him hard, for all I was worth, in the pit of his stomach. He was caught offguard, dropped me and I made for the beach as fast as I could scramble out.

'You're back soon,' Mother said, as I flopped down and started to dry myself. I muttered something about the water being cold then I picked up my spade and started to dig a speedboat. I dug as if my life depended on it. I'd had enough of being grown-up for the moment.

*

I opened one eye and saw my new navy gym-slip hanging on the wardrobe door and my underwear neatly piled on the chair where Mother had left it. It was no good making a fuss about the combinations and liberty bodice. At least I had cast the chest protector. Then I noticed the knickers and screamed. Mother had not bought the regulation navy bloomers but knitted them in four-ply. In answer to my roar of indignation, she put her head round the door.

'Stop making such a fuss, there are some white linings, press-studded inside', as if that would mollify me. I was in a hurry so had no option but to pull the cumbersome lot up and get on with it.

'Don't forget to have some breakfast', Mother called up from the kitchen. I got my own back by rushing out of the house without eating anything. I'd be ravenous by eleven.

As I ran towards Roundhay Road, my clumsy underwear adding inches to my hips and chafing my thighs, I was kicking myself for not having noticed the knitting Mother had been occupied with lately. I could have throttled her. But I'd be alright as long as I didn't have to undress. The thought of that curdled my blood.

The autumn sun was pleasantly warm as I climbed up Gledhow Wood Road and my spirits rose. There was no need to walk on the footpath, as there were only two or three cars passing by at any time of day. There was a deep wooded gorge on the other side of the railings. The route was a big improvement on Harehills Lane. In the hall, after Prayers, Miss Vyvyan gave an address which went right over my head, all about character building and what she hoped for from her 'gels'. Then we were taken to our classroom and met our form mistress, Miss Hodgson, who was youngish, pleasant and taught history.

The first surprise was that at regular intervals during the day a bell rang and a different teacher, robes flying in the breeze, swept in. We all started from scratch in algebra and geometry which gave me an even bigger pain than arithmetic. Miss Rose, the maths mistress, further salted the wound by never learning my name. For the rest of my schooldays, she rechristened me Olga, which had the whole class serenading me behind her back with

'Olga Poloffski, the beautiful spy.' Every time I told Miss Rose my name, she looked astonished as if convinced I was mistaken.

That first day, we were taken to the gymnasium where Miss Sproat told us to undress down to our blouses and knickers. I nearly died from embarrassment. Needless to say, no-one else wore knitted underwear. There were several sidelong glances and amused gleams which were not helped by my lack of ability to perform on any apparatus. Two steps up the rope ladder and I felt terrified. I longed for a safety net. Vaulting over the horse was a nightmare. My body refused to obey any instructions from my brain. I had the same trouble with the parallel bars. My wrists, the only dainty part of me, lacked the strength to heave my body over.

Miss Sproat was fortyish with greasy, shingled brown hair, eyes of granite, a straight mouth, muscles of iron, and the determination that no twelve-year-old should best her. She grabbed my arm and manhandled me into somersaulting over the bars. At the end of the lesson I had bruises the size of tea plates.

Back home that evening before we had tea, I mutinied.

'I am not going to wear those knickers again. Under any circumstances!' I stormed at Mother. Then I sat down and waited for the sky to fall in. To my astonishment, Mother waved the white flag and surrendered. Perhaps tackling grown-ups might not be so daunting after all.

There wasn't a trace of lipstick or powder on any staff face. 'Perhaps make-up is taboo in schools, like married women,' Mother said. Then why had we to take pocket mirrors to our next French lesson? The mystery was soon solved when mirrors in hand, we practised our French vowels, pursing our lips as Miss Appleyard demonstrated. We were more farmyard than Sorbonne. Our accents never improved much as Miss Appleyard, despite her fluency, spoke French with a marked

Yorkshire accent. She also provided us with the best moment of the week when, at hometime, we saw her cycling down the hill, her short sturdy lisle-clad legs going like pistons. She wore a homemade flowered cotton frock, with a V-shaped neck which was not quite symmetrical. Her light brown hair, centre parted, hung like two crimped curtains topped by a blue velour helmet. Her eyes, behind gold-rimmed specs, were focused intently on a far horizon. Given a spear, she could have doubled for Boadicea, pedalling into battle.

Our laughter might have been kinder, had we known Miss Appleyard was the mainstay of a poverty-stricken family. She had no change out of her seven pounds a week for clothes or any other frivolities.

There were so many things to learn that my head was whirling. Botany had me at a disadvantage because the other girls had learnt the names of wild flowers in their first years at primary school and the teacher, Miss Rankin, was no help. She was tall, with fair Marcel-waved hair anchored by a velvet band halfway down her forehead. I later decided this must have stopped the flow of blood to her memory, for when she set us homework, she kept it for months and then forgot to mark it. Fortunately we soon moved on to frogs which I found more interesting, although I detested the smell of formaldehyde used for preserving them. After dissecting one for an entire lesson, I felt sick and was glad to escape into the fresh air.

On reaching home there were my favourite egg sandwiches waiting on the kitchen table. 'Hullo, Mum!' I said, as I commenced to wolf them down. Then I dropped the food with a moan. The smell of formaldehyde and frogs was rising from my sandwich. I'd forgotten to wash my hands.

'The French eat frogs,' Mother said with a laugh. That finished me off altogether.

Once a week, we had a cookery lesson with Miss Green, a sharp-nosed martinet, who specialised in rock buns. As tasting and talking were forbidden, the lessons were as heavy going as the baking. Then there was Miss White, the sewing mistress, a little dormouse of a woman in a tussore shirt, man's tie, woollen stockings and lace-up shoes, the outfit popular with most of our teachers.

Our first lesson with Miss White was on how to make a sewing bag in which to hold our term's work. I sat there, expecting to make a linen envelope like a nightdress case. Instead, we were given sheets of thick brown paper and told how to fold them. Surely we should then paste the pieces together?

'Er, no.' Miss White looked anguished at the thought. 'Unfortunately in the past, whenever we used paste, it attracted mice who loved the flavour and ate every bag in the cupboard!' We had to blanket-stitch the brown paper. Things did not improve. For the rest of the term we made dirndl skirts from red checked material. They were so horrible that even the slim girls swore they wouldn't be seen dead in them.

Our Latin teacher, Miss Cowling, was tall, heavily built, with large, yellow teeth, a sallow complexion, and hair scraped back into a bun. In her mannish outfit, she looked what she was, a dragon. I never managed to please her. After a session with her, Art classes were a relief as at least I could draw. Unfortunately, Miss Wright, the teacher, loved nothing better than an orange and apple still life, a subject more boring than laburnum. I soon discovered Miss Wright's true vocation was as a medical artist. She spent hours in a hospital theatre, looking over Lord Moynihan's shoulder and portraying the operation in progress in oils. These paintings were used to illustrate text books.

I worked very hard at all the subjects in a damp haze of anxiety for most of the time. I was in a B form but the end of year exams would decide which class I should stay in. If I were in the bottom layer, I should be branded a dunce, go into the C form and be sentenced to another three years of hewing rock buns and sewing brown paper. I began to feel as tense as before the scholarship exam.

On the last day of term, Miss Hodgson read out the results. Violet was top of the class. No surprise there, she was brilliant. Margaret, who was equally clever, had come second. Both shone at mathematics, lucky pair! The next name gave me a jolt of delight — it was mine! My other marks had made up for my maths. I was going up into an A form. Keeping up the standard would always be difficult but I was thrilled.

At the end of my first year at Roundhay, I had only two big hates: Miss Sproat and gymnastics. I had made no progress and had the bruises to prove it. Also I was shy of communal nudity in the showers. Much to Miss Sproat's disgust, I clung to my swimsuit. I also disliked hockey nearly as much as gym. My idea of misery was a damp, freezing spell spent bullying-off on the pitch. Once I annoyed Miss Sproat by chatting to another girl instead of concentrating on the game, and on another occasion I hit the ball into the wrong goal and spent the rest of the period in disgrace, walking round the pitch. Here I pondered, would no-one rid me of this troublesome female? Someone did. Miss Sproat did the totally unexpected. She left to get married!

*

It was the first day of the autumn term and as I puffed up Gledhow Wood Road, I wondered who would be our form mistress for the coming year. It was not long before I heard the dread news. It was Miss Cowling.

She cast a baleful eye over us, especially me. 'Put your

belongings including the contents of your shoe bags out on your desks, so that I can see if everything is marked.'

Oh, calamity! I'd forgotten my shoe bag. I started to stammer out an excuse but Miss Cowling cut me short with, 'You're plausible. But bring it here this afternoon.'

'But, Miss Cowling, I'm staying for school dinner.'

'Then bring it back this evening after school.'

At four o'clock I had to run home, grab the bag, then gallop back to the staff room where it was inspected. I was then dismissed with a bleak nod.

All the way home I brooded on why Miss Cowling had labelled me 'plausible.' I had not told any lie. She was obviously 'anti', but anti-what? Perhaps she wished to improve my character, in line with Miss Vyvyan's sermons. But whatever her reason I never forgot my shoe bag again.

The Jewish girls were only obliged to attend morning prayers on the first day of the term. For the rest of the time we stayed in our form rooms and therefore missed most of Miss Vyvyan's sermons. I doubt whether that term's first address was typical. She had admonished the school, 'When gels go into the toilet, on no account must they go in two at a time.' Apart from conjuring up a vision of the Ark, this seemingly irrelevant bit of advice nonplussed us all and I put it down to the vagaries of schoolmarms.

Everyone in our class went to the lavatory 'in penny numbers', as Marjory put it, except the two Bettys. Known as Thin Betty and Ginger Betty, they went in together to continue chatting about their homework. I'd heard them. It all seemed innocent to me.

Ginger Betty, a round-faced, bonny girl with flame-coloured hair, was not at school the following day. Or the next day. No-one remarked on it as it was assumed she was a victim of the measles epidemic. We were shocked to hear a week later that Betty with her friendly smile and fiery hair, had contracted meningitis and died. I half associated her death with going to the lavatory with her friend but Miss Vyvyan never raised the subject again and no-one ever enlightened us.

*

I found being excused assembly very useful as I could spend the extra quarter of an hour or so polishing up my homework. Most times, when Mother checked whether I had done it properly, I said, 'Oh, I can learn that tomorrow during prayers.' So I was dumbfounded to find at nine am one morning, when I was in the classroom about to go over a bit of Ovid, that some well-meaning Rabbi had petitioned for facilities to be provided for separate prayers for the Jewish pupils.

I wished him no good when I was told to repair immediately to the Library, Latin homework undone. We were supervised by a Jewish prefect, poor girl. Most of us were noisy and full of fun, without any staff around, and the next quarter of an hour was no exception. None of the girls seemed in the mood for prayer so after a few minutes' attention to a passage from the Old Testament, our gathering of about twenty girls split up into little groups for a gossip. It was like a lively mothers' meeting.

I was already friendly with Little Anita, the only other Jewish girl in my class. That first day of Jewish prayers I met Big Anita, who, as well as being six inches taller than Little Anita, was also larger than life — an attractive brunette, with a big bust, small waist, wicked gleam in her dark eyes, and a natural attraction for the opposite sex. At fifteen, she was a year ahead of me in more ways than one.

As our friendship progressed, I owed the most useful

bits of my education to the two Anitas. Big Anita changed boyfriends weekly and her love life was a lot more interesting than the gods and nymphs of Ovid. We were both trying to diet as the puppyfat was threatening to cling forever. I had been taken that week into Hitchens, where Mother had bought me a pair of boned, laced-up stays. I had endured them all the weekend but knew they were going to defeat me. Worldly Big Anita advised Marshall and Snelgroves' sales. 'They sell zip-sided, two-way stretch girdles.' And the best tip of all, 'Ruddock brassieres — they'll point you up in the right direction!' After such advice we'd hear what her latest boyfriend had attempted to do last night, the saucy bits punctuated by peals of laughter.

Big Anita's surname was Brook, so her giggle, which could be heard a mile away, caused her to be re-christened Babbling. I wouldn't have missed Jewish prayers for anything even if I now had to do all my homework at home. Thank Heaven no member of the staff was Jewish!

Little Anita was also streets ahead of me in sophistication, although she was in my year. She had an older sister who wore model clothes. So did Anita when her sister wasn't looking. Not that Little Anita excelled as a needlewoman; when she inherited a dress which was much too long, she chopped three inches off, then wore it with a raw hem.

Anita 'borrowed' a book from her sister and was suddenly the most popular girl in the class. The book was a novel, *The Priceless Pearl*, and it was harmless but hilariously pornographic. The heroine valued her Priceless Pearl so much that after every love affair she had it re-stitched!

Little Anita's older brother was an excellent ballroom dancer and had taught Anita to waltz, foxtrot, rumba and tango like a Latin American. None of our form could do so much as a simple chassis. 'We'll soon change that,' said Anita. With the confidence of a Napoleon, she marshalled us into the corridor at every break for dancing lessons. Someone, generally Marjory Pilbeam, who was felt to have no future as a Ginger Rogers, stood on guard at the end of the corridor. Combs and tissue paper provided the orchestra. I was excused orchestral duties as Anita was also musical.

Some of us had as much natural grace as baby elephants but Anita was determined and cracked the whip with perfect rhythm. 'One-two! Stretch your legs straight out behind you. And bring your feet together or you'll look as if you've wet yourself!'

To the music of *Blue Skies, I'll See You In My Dreams*, and *Jealousy*, Anita partnered us each in turn, trying to ignore how much our busts got in the way. With 'Dip and glide, keep those legs straight! Now to one side…feet together!' she steered us, none too gently, the full length of our corridor, with intent faces, gymslips twirling and elbows shoulder high. It was better than gym any day. Fortunately our classroom was at the side of the building so we escaped detection by the skin of our palais glides.

Marjory only let us down once. She was distracted by the rest of us collapsing into fits of laughter at the sight of Little Anita, four feet eleven, tangoing with six-feet-tall Annie. Annie's bust was resting on Anita's head. Never in the history of ballroom dancing have so many hefty girls melted away as quickly as that time when Miss Vyvyan swept round the corner. Much to our astonishment, nothing was said. Word must have circulated around the staff about our extra-curricular activity as no-one ever came round the corner again without giving a warning cough. I cherished the thought that Miss Vyvyan might have wanted to learn ballroom dancing when she was young.

Anita only called a halt to dancing lessons when we

were pronounced fit for the ballroom. When the time came, I never took to the floor without remembering her ringing tones, 'For goodness' sake, keep your feet together!' Hers was the most useful lesson I ever had at school.

Chapter Six

I stood with the other beginners at the corner of the Palais dance floor. The band was playing *Deep Purple* and a chap with a Ronald Colman moustache and glossy hair approached, twitched an eyebrow in my direction and swept me off, gliding and twirling, until the music stopped. Then he escorted me back to the starting post and whisked someone else away without saying a word.

Learners' Night cost sixpence but was value for money as my dancing had improved, and also there was no danger of being a wallflower or having to make boring conversation, such as 'Do you come here often?'

I was only fourteen but Mother did not mind me going and the freedom was heady. I was itching to spread my wings further so I joined the Young Zionists. Not for the dances, they were a dead loss, as only the girls could dance. The boys just leaned against the walls, looking bored. I never minded dancing with a girl when there were no boys around but hated it in mixed company. Perhaps we should have sent Little Anita round to their school.

The dances might have been poor but the meetings were great fun especially when we had a speaker. I was totally ignorant of any background history of the Zionist movement or of anything to do with Palestine. To my shame, it was many years before it dawned on me that Israel was once the land of Canaan, the site of my favourite Bible stories.

My head was mainly filled with the boys I was meeting and which one would walk me home. They were all at Central High school in the sixth form. When I wanted to impress anyone I fibbed about my age.

I had little choice of clothes for my socialising but this

also applied to my friends. The boys mostly wore blazers and flannels. Those who had fathers in the tailoring trade had overcoats 'cut to grow into' which reached nearly down to the ground. Dad let me have a dress from his stock and I picked a black one. The magazines all advised 'A little black dress would see you through' and although we laughed, we obeyed just the same. Stockings were a constant worry as pure silk at two-and-eleven was too expensive for more than special occasions. Instead, I made do with one-and-eleven-penny rayon stockings turned inside out to dim the shine. As they were not fully-fashioned, I had to cut off the fringe round the ankles; a tricky operation, for too close a cut meant a hole and ladders before they had ever been worn.

Mother was surprisingly broadminded about high heels and I was allowed to wear them away from school. We went into Timpsons' one Saturday morning for a pair of really smart suede shoes. 'Quite reasonable, for seven-and-six,' Mother said. When I stood up to try them on, my coat caught a huge display of shoes on glass panels, supported by glass columns. In slow motion the whole pyramid came crashing down. There was broken glass everywhere. 'I'm so sorry!' Mother gasped to the ashen-faced assistant, then hissed to me, 'Do they fit you? If so, let's get out of here!' The seven-and-six changed hands in record time and we ran. I never dared go into Timpsons' again.

I was longing to wear make-up but Mother wouldn't hear of it. She possessed a Tangee lipstick for weddings and Barmitzvahs but only lent it to me for an occasional daub. Eventually I smuggled in a pillar-box red lipstick from Woolworth's with a threepenny box of Betty-Lou powder. I could not afford anything else but my cheeks were red enough. My eyebrows were like a forest, however, so after an illicit snoop in Mother's dressing table drawer, I found some tweezers and pruned myself down. I took care not to make them into a Marlene Dietrich thin line and outrage Mother. A touch of vaseline and a matchstalk full of soot from my bedroom chimney for my eyelashes, and I was ready to go out. Unfortunately, just as I called 'I'm off!' Dad came out of the kitchen and caught me.

'Go and wash all that muck off your face! No daughter of mine is going out looking like a tart with painted eyebrows!' He'd taken exception to the one bit of my face that was au naturel! I went back upstairs, rubbed a bit of Betty-Lou off, then escaped.

Provided I soft-pedalled the lipstick, nothing was ever said again. Eventually Mother also started wearing lipstick, and beads, which she had hitherto condemned as common.

As well as experimenting with make-up, I was always trying new hairstyles. After a shampoo and a vinegar rinse, every strand was pin-curled into worm-casts, anchored by a criss-cross of kirby grips. When I was going dancing in the evening, I went to school with my hair still pin-curled. Miss Rose once stopped Little Anita, whose hair was similar to mine and asked her how she managed it. After listening to a brief explanation, Miss Rose went on her way down the corridor, awestruck, muttering, 'Amazing!'

Sometimes I went out to lunch with Mother on Saturday with all the ironmongery still in place. I looked nearly as bad as the girls we were accustomed to seeing walking two abreast down Briggate, in identical evening dresses but with their hair in curlers.

Mixing with boys at the club inevitably led to parties, which were clandestine and held wherever there was a parentless house available. All the boys had in mind was kissing games. 'Sorry! can't talk until I've cleaned my teeth' I moaned to Mother after one party, 'I've been kissed all the evening, and feel sick!' Mother received this account of my ill-spent evening with bemused tolerance, yet sobbed and threatened never to forgive me because I now preferred going out with my girl friends to her.

I had no special boy friend until I met Alfred. He was a tall, quiet, studious boy, a newcomer to the club, who had not been to any of the parties. His shyness appealed to me as I was also tongue-tied with boys. It never occurred to me that one reason there was so much kissing at the parties might have been because none of us had any idea how to make conversation!

When Alfred asked me out I was fifteen and it was my first date. I was excited yet scared. Was this funny feeling love and how was I supposed to act? Pocket money was short all round so dates never amounted to anything more than a walk in the park. 'Look out if he's got a raincoat and a newspaper,' Big Anita laughed, when I told her at school.

Alfred had fourpence for tram fares to the Park and there was no sign of the *Yorkshire Evening Post* in his mac pocket so I relaxed. It was a lovely summer's evening and the Gorge smelt of bracken and distant garden fires. We sat down on his mac. He smiled, said nothing, then kissed me. It was strange without the other giggling boys and girls in the background. Then he undid the top press stud of my dress and a warning signal sounded in my head.

'I think I'd better be going,' I muttered. Neither of us said a word as he walked me home and he did not kiss me at the gate. I couldn't sleep at all that night, I felt so muddled. I had fallen out of love as quickly as I had fallen in.

At the club the next evening, when Alfred came bounding over to claim me and I cut him dead, I could no more have explained why than discussed the Theory of Relativity. Alfred looked very upset but we never spoke to each other again.

Yet my head was still full of romance. I had my nose in Ethel M Dell, Ursula Bloom and Denise Robbins all the time. At an earthier level, school work was enlivened by an epidemic of dirty jokes circulating round the upper forms and swapped during Jewish Prayers. If I could find a double entendre in any conversation, I did.

During Miss Muriel's English lesson, which was on *The Song Of Solomon,* I found something salacious in every line and kept turning round and smirking at Anita. 'My beloved is unto me as a cluster of camphor,' had me grinning over my shoulder again. It was once too often for Miss Muriel who was a plump, motherly woman with grey wispy curls, a warm smile and beaming eyes. She had a rare gift for teaching and inspiring affection. We took advantage of her sometimes by digressing but she seemed to enjoy it, and our work was none the poorer for discussing topics other than syntax. I was very fond of her.

Her smile disappeared and her face saddened. 'Girls!' she clapped her hands together. 'You must stop this suggestive sniggering about such beautiful love poetry. Sex and love combined are to be respected and not belittled by dirty talk.'

Miss Muriel continued tearing a strip off all of us but, in the main, keeping her eye on me. I felt myself blushing scarlet and tears were not far away. I was ashamed down to my feet, especially as I could appreciate the power and beauty of the poetry. My smirking had defiled it. And I had upset my favourite teacher.

Darling that she was, Miss Muriel forgave us all and the next day invited the class to her home for tea on Saturday. We were treated to dainty sandwiches, homemade cakes and adult conversation. It was bliss.

But despite Miss Muriel's homily and a surfeit of romantic novels, I had no real guidelines for my social life. At the next party I was invited to, I was with a new boy friend, Selig, and we had the front room to ourselves. I was sitting on his lap and he was kissing me. He was an intelligent, good looking boy but I felt nothing like any of the heroines I'd been reading about. No bells rang; neither did my heart beat faster. I sat up.

'I don't love you,' I blurted out. He too sat up, so abruptly that I nearly fell off his lap.

'I don't love you, either! What's that got to do with it?'

That was the end of that friendship. I spent another sleepless night, kicking myself for being such a silly fool. It was not the last time I should toss and turn for the same reason and lie there wondering what to make of it all.

*

My excitement was intense as I watched my new bedroom furniture being carried upstairs. I stroked the glossy finish of the bird's eye maple, with the scrolled walnut handles, then put my clothes away and locked my diary and other treasures inside the desk. It was my fifteenth birthday present from Mother and Dad. We had gone up to London to choose it from Uncle Aaron's workroom. His craftsmanship was superb.

'The whole lot will set Joe back twenty-five pounds,' Uncle Aaron had told Mother. The enormity of the gift made me hug her, especially as my room had been decorated to my own taste; cream paper and paint, with a beige carpet and matching lino. All the rest of the house had dark brown woodwork except the bathroom, which was bottle green, and the kitchen, an acre of maroon.

My room was heated by a bowl radiator, plugged into an adaptor in the light socket and controlled by an on-off button. The bowl was kept beside the tallboy in the alcove when not in use. Two days after the furniture arrived, I put the bedroom light on, then went downstairs to look for a book. Suddenly I smelled something burning, the pungent searing of polished wood. I raced up the stairs, two at a time. I had forgotten to switch off the radiator. It was sizzling my new tallboy, burning an area as big as a dinner plate.

Dad was out, thank Heaven! But Mother made up for it. She was livid, understandably, yet it never occurred to her that the heating in my room was potentially lethal. We could have all gone up in smoke.

'You'll have to pay for the repair,' Mother snapped. It wasn't the cost. I was upset that something so beautiful should have been ruined by my own carelessness. Also the prospect of Dad's reaction terrified me. He had to work hard enough for his money without me burning it. As if she were reading my mind, Mother softened. 'I'll try and get Denby and Spinks to collect the tallboy on Monday, when your father's gone off for the week. With luck, he might not find out.'

True to her promise, she arranged it, and miraculously the tallboy was returned as good as new on Friday before Dad came home. It set my savings back by twenty-five shillings but it was worth it. The repair was so skilfully done I couldn't find it and, what was even better, Dad never found out either.

School also had a couple of shocks that summer. Miss Vyvyan was leaving because of ill health. And so was Miss Muriel, who had reached retirement age.

Miss Nixon was to be the new headmistress, although, as rumour had it, she had been a buyer at Lewis's. 'That's a funny background, for a headmistress,' I commented to Big Anita during our prayers. 'What on earth will she have learnt about schoolgirls, in Lewis's?' Not a lot, I soon found out.

I was sent to her office with the register one Friday morning, and she bit my head off for no reason as I went round the door. We took an instant dislike to each other, which unfortunately never changed.

Miss Muriel's replacement was Miss Cryer, who was only in her thirties but far older in her ways than her predecessor. Her hair was fair, long and dressed in a bun like that of all our more stolid academics. She was small and slim, tilting her head up like a bird as she recited her favourite poems; her mouth pursed and face flushed from the pleasure she found from listening to her own voice, which to my mind was mincingly affected. But despite that, I paid attention and kept up my standard although I no longer enjoyed English lessons.

My sixteenth birthday came and went. Mother announced she and Dad were going to Birmingham for another of Uncle Lewin's parties and I could ask Little Anita to stay overnight with me. She accepted with alacrity.

When we arrived home from school, Anita was most impressed by our latest acquisition, a 'fridge, an almost unheard-of luxury in an ordinary household. Mother had answered an advertisement for it in the *Yorkshire Evening Post*. It had belonged to a Mr May, a wealthy gentleman living in a mansion. The butler was in charge of the transaction and Mother was most impressed that she had dealt with a real live butler. The 'fridge was six feet tall, three feet wide and with four doors, all in solid oak with huge chrome hinges. It filled an alcove in our kitchen. The wiring went through a hole in the wall into the pantry and from there into the coal house, where the engine, like an outboard motor, was sited. It was a bit noisy but worked perfectly and is probably still going strong. Mother had a bargain for five pounds.

Mother had left plenty of food for us, herring, fish and jelly and custard. Not yet used to a refrigerator, she had not covered up any of the food so even the custard tasted of herring.

Anita and I had nothing more exciting planned than a Young Zionist meeting, where there was a debate, 'Should women take more interest in politics?' It was a lively discussion but to no great point. In a man's world, no woman could ever hope to become Prime Minister.

Two students I did not know well walked us home. I invited them in and, anxious to impress, set the tea tray with Mother's best china. It was translucent and decorated with a delicate lilac and gold pattern. Mother rarely, if ever, used her best things, something which always annoyed me.

We drank our tea in style and the four of us hit it off with so much badinage bouncing back and forth that we were helpless from laughter. We finished the evening dancing an Indian war dance before we said goodnight at a respectable eleven o'clock without any kissing. It had been a memorable evening. I put the tray of china squarely in the middle of the kitchen table before Anita and I fell into our respective beds.

The next morning we overslept so ran out of the house without having any breakfast. There would be plenty of time later for me to wash up and make the beds before Mother came back.

Anita had taken her things with her to school so I was alone when I returned home and walked into the kitchen. The tray was on the floor, with the china in smithereens, amongst spilt sugar and milk.

At first, I thought I was having a nightmare. Then I seriously wondered if there were a poltergeist around but dismissed this as too fanciful. As I picked up the tray I realised that if it had fallen off the table accidentally the contents would have spilled over the floor. They were all on the tray. It had been dropped. But not by me.

Would Mother believe me? I was in agony as I heard her key in the lock. Her smile evaporated quicker than the sun in November when she saw the debris. 'How dare you use my best china? It was a wedding present!' That did it. I sat down and buried my head in my hands. I felt as if I were going mad, the situation was so bizarre. Mother would not listen or believe that I had not broken the china. I had taken it without her permission, she said, so was responsible. I should have to pay for it to be repaired. The pieces were taken in to Awmacks and I had to fork out twenty-five shillings again. Twenty-five seemed to be my unlucky number.

Alice had a key to our house but Mother would not hear a word against her. I was the culprit and there was no more to be said. But Alice wore her deadpan expression all the time I told her about the breakage so I knew.

I didn't invite any boys back home again for a while. Instead, some used to congregate outside the gate, and sing *Miss Otis Regrets She's Unable To Lunch Today*, until Mother said, 'For goodness sake, go out to speak to your friends, they'll have the street up.' Whenever anyone walked me home at night the lamp outside our house was a terrible nuisance. Not only were we floodlit, but when Mother loomed at the bedroom window, the light shone on her white nightie, making her look like a demented ghost. Her tone was far from sepulchral as she called down in her best duchessy manner, 'That will do, Joan! Come in immediately!' At this, all the nearby curtains twitched.

One rainy night, all they would have been treated to when I thought I was looking glamorous, was the sight of my face striped like a zebra. My vaseline-and-soot mascara had run.

If I did invite my escort inside for the obligatory cuppa, Mother would eventually put her knitting away and go up to bed. At half past eleven, she rang the bell from her bedroom and that meant throwing-out time. Many years later, when a young man with serious intentions sat there, Mother rose, said goodnight then added, 'I'll ring the bell at eleven-thirty for the young man to leave, like I always do!' I never lived it down.

*

My parents continued to quarrel whenever they set eyes on each other. Mother did not help matters by sulking, convinced she was always the innocent party. Our family was not the only one suffering from disharmony. Mother received a letter from her sister Natalie in New York with cuttings from American papers alleging our King had a twice-divorced lady friend, whom he wished to marry. We could not believe it as there had been no mention of Mrs Simpson in our press. The day the letter arrived I went in to town. As I stood outside Lewis's, queueing for a number three tram, I saw a *Yorkshire Evening Post* placard — 'King abdicates'. I nearly missed the tram from shock.

At home we crowded round the radio to hear the King's farewell speech. We were only accustomed to a royal address on Christmas day. When the King said 'I cannot go on without the woman I love', it brought a lump to the throat. His abdication was the biggest Royal upheaval of the century. Everyone discussed the pros and cons, and the Prime Minister, Mr Baldwin, received more than his fair share of the blame. Edward was very popular with his blond hair, Windsor-knotted tie and concern for the miners. Although the monarchy may have wobbled for a moment, Queen Mary, stiff as a ramrod, was still there in the background to bolster it up.

Mother's view, despite her love for the monarchy, was shared by many. 'He hasn't done his duty,' she said. Duty was a much respected word in 1936.

My parents were living together from duty. 'I never

wanted you to suffer without a father like I had to,' Dad told me more than once. And the last words he ever spoke to me decades later were, 'You're a good girl and have always done your duty.' It was an accolade I didn't deserve but cherished more than any bequest.

The royal uproar eventually settled and I was back in the usual routine; working for matric at school and putting up with the rows at home. Two of my friends were faring even worse. Stick-thin Margaret had arrived home one afternoon to discover that her stepmother, who never cooked her a meal, had decamped with all the furniture. Margaret left school at the end of the year to help out.

Violet also confided her troubles to me. Her mother had become ill and needed an operation followed by lengthy treatment. An orphanage was asked to supply a girl to live in as a maid. When Violet's mother came out of hospital, she found the maid was pregnant and Violet's father was responsible. A divorce was looming, and Violet too would have to leave school. They were the cleverest girls in the class. I felt very sorry for them.

Anita and I were both worried about the approaching matriculation exams. So when we were told that during the Easter holidays there was a week's course in French at a boarding school in Pannal, near Harrogate, we leapt at it. Now was my chance, after years of Angela Brazil's school stories, to get a taste of the real thing.

The Headmistress received us at the door. She had a well-modulated voice with an Oxford accent which was, in Dad's words, 'Orf'lly cut-glarss.'

'It's a naice day,' she said to Dad as she ushered us in.

'It is indeed,' he replied, wickedly la-di-da,'in fact, we've hed a lot of weather lately,' and he doffed his bowler hat down to the ground, before adding, 'and Ay think we'll hev a lot more in the future!' If it were possible to die from embarrassment, I should have expired on the spot. But curiosity soon revived me.

Alas, Angela Brazil had not been to Pannal. The French lessons were too boring to be useful and it was obvious after the first meal that if Bessie Bunter had attended that school, she would have emerged a sylph. Breakfast consisted of a few cornflakes through which we could see the dish. Lunch found us looking at two cubes of meat and some soggy cabbage. Tea was also an exercise in belt-tightening, bread and marge and two cubes of tinned pineapple floating in a soup plate. The food marched in twos at that school.

Anita and I were too timid to do an Oliver Twist so at the first opportunity we made our way to Harrogate and spent two-and-six on a carrier bag full of biscuits and apples. We missed the bus and the route-march back to Pannal sharpened our appetites even more. My figure improved that week but not my French, and I was cured forever of reading boarding school stories.

Once I was home again, I spent the summer months swotting with one ear tuned in to Wimbledon. While I was memorising 'Qualis spelunca', I was also cheering Fred Perry on to his triumphs. The ping of the ball nicely punctuated the rhythm of the Latin. I sweated over theorems and mugged up on the French vocabulary with tennis in the background.

Before I knew it, I was wiping my sweating palms and sitting in the hall, tackling the Matriculation papers. I was lucky. One question was on the Latin I had memorised and I'd also learnt the right theorems.

We celebrated the end of term with a hen-party at Little Anita's as her family were conveniently away. There were seven of us from our form and we had each brought some food. The evening started sedately enough as we cut the cakes into seven portions, but the laughter escalated when each sardine and currant from the teacakes were shared out. We laughed so much at nothing in particular that when Anne rose up from her chair, she left a pool behind her. That evening was the highlight of whatever was carefree about my youth.

*

The world outside was beginning to intrude even through my self-centred skin, especially when I saw how many refugees from Germany and other European countries were seeking a new life in Leeds. Unfortunately, some were arrogant. Perhaps they needed to be to survive. They had certainly come from the most assimilated of Jewish communities, where conversion to Christianity, for expedience, was not uncommon. Many local bigots muttered, 'Their persecution is from God, for not having kept to the Faith'. I thought the devil was more likely responsible. The Vatican's view was that the Jews only had a problem because they would not become good Christians. In such a world the refugees had a lot to put up with.

Gerd, Helga and their mother were the first German refugees I met. Like me Helga was seventeen. She and her mother, although refined and educated, were working as domestic servants. Gerd had a menial job in a factory. These were the only jobs open to them. Gerd was an adaptable, lively young man, determined to enjoy and make the most of his life. During our conversations he did not describe how the Nazis had killed his father or speak of their own narrow escape. His mother and sister had sad eyes and roughened hands but they also did not complain. It was only when Helga showed me a photograph of herself and her family, standing by a large car in the grounds of a magnificent house, that I appreciated what they had left behind. Yet they were the lucky ones. They had their lives. Sitting looking at their photograph, in our comfortable, safe living-room, I shivered.

*

After I had matriculated, school was a bit of an anti-climax. Added to that I was beginning to worry as to what I should do when I left in two years' time. I dismissed the thought of teaching and by this immediately put myself further out of favour with Miss Nixon. She only showed interest in candidates for degree courses or teaching diplomas. There was no other guidance offered, not even a five minutes' interview. I was also concerned about the work involved for Higher School Certificate. French at the advanced level included the study of French Literature, which I was not sold on even when translated.

There was another problem. In my last year at school, I fell deeply in love and it was not the violin-playing, romantic experience I had been led to expect. Instead, it was a churning, burning, passionate feeling, which was bedevilled from the start. He was the brother of a friend and she was greatly put out by it. I never asked her why but the friendship was badly dented and this upset me. I was even more upset when Mother burst into my bedroom early one Sunday morning with the news that my boyfriend had been involved in an accident, driving a car with faulty brakes. He was alright but his passenger had been killed. She added, 'So under no circumstances can you go out with him again.'

Not many eighteen-year-olds heed that kind of challenge. That the meetings were clandestine added little zest to the relationship. I should have much preferred Mother to have encouraged the romance. But the only time he came to the house, she was so rude to him, he never came over the doorstep again. I could understand her fear for me but not her insulting behaviour. Dad sided with her so home became a prison where none of us communicated.

Although I continued to see Alan, I was desperately unhappy and my work at school suffered. I disliked the sixth form set-up where we only had a cubby-hole for a classroom and were expected to study alone in the library. It was a reasonable preparation for university life but not one that suited me. I missed the comradeship and competitive cut-and-thrust of class work. Also, my best subject, English, was now a nightmare, as Miss Cryer had chosen our exam syllabus without consulting us. She adored Chaucer and her cheeks were even rosier as she waxed lyrical in Olde Englishe. I was horrified. I only understood one word in ten but my protestations fell on deaf ears as Miss Cryer was deliriously happy. It never occured to her to tell us that there was a good translation available in the Reference Library. I only found it two days before I was to sit the exam.

My school work was at a standstill. I had previously been a good student but no-one seemed to remember that, or ask me why my work had deteriorated. It was assumed I had just become bone idle. If I could have unburdened to somebody, I might have been able to cope better. The atmosphere at home was so awful that I made up my mind to try and get in to London University, where there was a two-year course in journalism. Matriculation was sufficient qualification so I was accepted.

Without telling my parents, I went to see the Midland Bank manager, to negotiate a loan against my inheritance from Grandpa. It was granted. The four hundred pounds would comfortably see me through two years in London.

When I told Mother, she was heartbroken. She cried non-stop. Our home, now a guilt-filled battle zone, reflected the outside world. Hitler was pointing his guns across Europe and twisting our stomachs with fear. Austria had been taken. Czechoslovakia and Poland were trembling. When war seemed a horrific probability, Mr Chamberlain, the Prime Minister, went to Munich and tried to deflect Hitler from his madness. On his return, waving a piece of paper from the top of the aircraft steps, Mr Chamberlain said 'I believe it is peace in our time.'

We all breathed more freely but war was brought home to us at school by the issue of gas masks. When we practised wearing them, there was no joking or laughter. It was a claustrophobic experience I was not anxious to repeat.

In the meantime, our next door neighbours, Jack and Alice, seemed cooler towards us. Mother refused to see it until we noticed that whenever we had been out, we found the phone replaced on the cradle the other way round. Alice still had the key to our house.

At last Mother realised that her friend was not all she seemed. Alice was undoubtedly using our phone without paying for long-distance calls to her sister. Mother, on the other hand, had no intention of economising and then giving Dad a large bill for calls she had not made. She said nothing to Alice about it but asked her for the key to be returned. There were no more visits, just a nod and a 'Good morning' when necessary.

Alice took her own revenge. Every time Dad reversed the car out of the garage, she sent the dog out; it then barked in a frenzy, running in and out from under the wheels. It was taking Dad twice as long to back down the drive to go to work. Finally he had had enough of it. He rang their bell and asked Alice in a polite manner to keep their dog under better control or he could not be responsible for its safety.

Jack came to the door, his heavy face flushed with rage and pushing Alice aside, screamed at the top of his voice, 'You bloody dirty Jew! You and the rest of your lot all ought to be wiped off the face of this earth! Hitler should burn the lot of you!' There was more in the same vein as Father stood transfixed. Then the door was slammed in his face.

Mother and I, in the kitchen, overheard and saw it all. Dad hesitated for a moment then grey-faced, turned on his heel and came back inside. He went straight to the phone.

'I'm afraid he's a rabid anti-semite,' I heard him say 'and would like Hitler to murder us all...Yes, I thought you'd feel the same.'

Jack had forgotten that he worked for a Jewish firm. The next day when he went to work he was sacked.

*

Then my love affair ended. I had seen it coming but had hoped against hope. I became impossible to live with and near to a breakdown. Only the thought of my forthcoming university course kept me going. At the end of July, I shook hands with Miss Nixon, who muttered a curt farewell with no good wishes.

Now I was leaving school. At nineteen, I'd had more than enough of it, although I have always regretted wasting my last two years there. As I ran out of the school gates, swinging my satchel for the last time, the irony escaped me that I was better pleased at leaving than I had been on entering, six years previously. I tried not to think of what lay ahead. It would be an adventure, however it turned out.

All the way down the hill I wondered what I had done

to antagonise Miss Nixon. This would bother me whenever I thought of my time at Roundhay. Then many years later I had an eye-opener. I was on a train, travelling first-class on an expenses-paid trip and saw Miss Nixon pass by on her way to a second class compartment. As she had recognised me, and I felt sorry for her travelling on her own, I went along to pay my respects. Before I could say one word, she snapped, 'What on earth are you doing, travelling 'First'? You must be made of money!'

NEW BOOKS
FROM YORKSHIRE ART CIRCUS

If you have enjoyed this book, why not get another good read from Yorkshire Art Circus? You can order our books in any bookshop or write direct to Yorkshire Art Circus, FREEPOST LS2336, Castleford, West Yorkshire WF10 4BR. Please make cheques payable to Yorkshire Art Circus Ltd. If you order one book only please add £1.50 to cover postage and packing; if you order two or more books, postage is free. If you prefer to use an ACCESS or VISA credit card please ring 0977 603028 and we will take your order immediately. Please quote order reference JG/91.

SAFE HOUSE
Diane Tingle £4.99
ISBN 0 947780 63 7

Diane is a successful chef in a busy city restaurant, juggling the demands of work with the demands of bringing up children on her own. But within two months her confidence is shattered by violence. In this remarkable story Diane overcomes grief, fear and poverty to rebuild her sense of identity, and make a home for her family.
"Powerful stuff" Radio 4, Kaleidoscope

ON EARTH TO MAKE THE NUMBERS UP
and IN OUR BACKS
Evelyn Haythorne £4.99
ISBN 0 947780 58 0

"Sometimes," said Evelyn's mum ,"I think God only put me on this earth to make the numbers up." Evelyn is growing up fast in wartime South Yorkshire, facing the means test, the Parish Board and illness in the family. *In Our Backs* moves from autobiography to fiction, taking the story into the 1950s and creating a whole cast of Chaucer Street characters.

Evelyn Haythorne is one of Yorkshire's best loved writers and Yorkshire Art Circus is proud to re-issue her two books in a single volume.